HOW AMERICA MET THE JEWS

Program in Judaic Studies
Brown University
Box 1826
Providence, RI 02912

BROWN JUDAIC STUDIES

Edited by

Mary Gluck
David C. Jacobson
Maud Mandel
Saul M. Olyan
Rachel Rojanski
Michael L. Satlow
Adam Teller
Nelson Vieira

Number 360
HOW AMERICA MET THE JEWS

by
Hasia Diner

HOW AMERICA
MET THE JEWS

Hasia Diner

Brown Judaic Studies
Providence, Rhode Island

Library of Congress Cataloging-in-Publication Data

Names: Diner, Hasia R., author.
Title: How America met the Jews / by Hasia R. Diner.
Description: Providence, RI : Brown Judaic Studies, [2017] | Series: Brown
    Judaic Studies ; Number 360 | From the 1820s through the 1920s, nearly
    ninety percent of all Jews who left Europe moved to the United States. In
    this new book from Hasia Diner, she focuses on the realities of race,
    immigration, color, money, economic development, politics, and religion in
    America that shaped its history and made it such an attractive destination
    for Jews. Additionally, she approaches the question from the perspective
    of an America that sought out white immigrants to help stoke economic
    development and that valued religion as a force for morality. These
    tendencies converged and provided a situation where Jews could experience
    life in ways impossible elsewhere. | Includes bibliographical references
    and index.
Identifiers: LCCN 2017045069 (print) | LCCN 2017046526 (ebook) | ISBN
    9781946527035 (ebook) | ISBN 9781946527028 (pbk. : alk. paper) | ISBN
    9781946527042 (hardcover : alk. paper)
Subjects: LCSH: Jews—United States—History. | Immigrants—United
    States—History. | United States—Emigration and immigration—History. |
    United States—Ethnic relations.
Classification: LCC E184.35 (ebook) | LCC E184.35 .D54 2017 (print) | DDC
    973/.04924—dc23
LC record available at https://lccn.loc.gov/2017045069

Printed on acid-free paper.

Contents

Preface

This volume owed its immediate origins to a talk I gave at Brown University as part of its annual Brown Judaic Studies Lecture Series in the fall of 2016. It had a somewhat longer history, as I had actually begun thinking about this topic during the year 2004–2005 when I participated, along with so many of my colleagues in the field of American Jewish history, in a frenzy of community and scholarly programs organized in order to mark the 350th anniversary of Jewish life in America. A celebratory tone understandably suffused most of those events, even the ones that took place in university settings. Indeed many of the programs gathered together a coalition of scholars along with several Jewish community organizations and notable individuals under the rubric of "Celebrate 350."

For reasons, not particularly important here, my scholarly antennae bristled every time I confronted that word "celebrate," believing then, as now, that the historian's task involves striving for distance, questioning, probing, and not cheerleading for any group of people, any institution, or a particular nation state. I found that in many of those symposia my talk tended to sound the single discordant, maybe even slightly cynical, note as I asked my audiences to take off their party hats and to think about the three-and-a-half centuries not as an expression of the sterling qualities of either America or the Jews but as something that had been contingent on a set of circumstances that had nothing to do with merit, quality, or achievements of either.

I suggested instead that they consider how certain realities of American life met the particular experiences that Jews had encountered elsewhere. These two encountered each other and fashioned a particular kind of history.

The opportunity to lecture at Brown, a tremendous honor for which I thank Professor Rachel Rojanski, provided a chance, long after the festivities had stopped, to go back to the subject, this time to speak to an audience not interested in the whirlwind of congratulations but rather dedicated to a more analytic look at an important subject.

Brown's request to expand the lecture, together with the notes I had based on a small seminar with graduate students and faculty, into a slim book gave me an even more focused opportunity to think about this subject, about how American conditions and Jewish circumstances collided to produce a history. It has allowed me to think about it in greater depth and with, I hope, even greater distance than "Celebrate 350" had afforded.

Distance does not mean dispassion. Expanding the few hours of talk into a volume between two covers convinced me even more that by studying the Jews in light of American culture, broadly conceived, our understanding of American history becomes richer, deeper, and more complicated. I came away from this exercise with a firm conviction that scholars of American history, whether interested in economic, social, political, or cultural themes, would be well served by pausing, even if briefly, to think about the experiences of the millions of Jews who immigrated to America and encountered its realities.

The chance to expand the lecture into a book, short as it is, also led me to see, with more certainty than I had before, that when looking across the long arc of Jewish history, the American part of that story stands in a category of its own, that we can think of it as *sui generis.* That statement hovers around the uncomfortable and unprovable idea of American exceptionalism, a theme that disturbs and vexes historians, who rightly shy away from it. Two different issues shadow it, make it problematic, and for the most part have caused American historians to jettison it completely.

It assumes that the histories of Canada, Australia, New Zealand, Germany, Argentina, Korea, and so on have been carefully analyzed, point by point, in relationship to American history or some aspect of it, and that after meticulous data collection and analysis, the United States can in fact be said to have been exceptional, different, and unlike any other place. For the most part those who have blithely employed exceptionalism as a category, whether directly or indirectly, have actually never done that real detailed comparative work and have offered their statements about "special" or "unique" American phenomena without any real evidence at their command.

Exceptionalism also bears the taint of triumphalism, and many who have invoked it, whether American historians in the past or politicians in the present, have done so boastfully, with America being hailed as the best among all others. Singing the praises of democracy, liberty, independence, and bounty has for the most part involved brushing aside and ignoring slavery, racial segregation, violence, imperialism, and rapacious capitalism, all ever-present realities that bubbled through American history.

For all of these reasons I am not comfortable with assertions of exceptionalism in any sense of the word. But I am, after the writing of this book as well as after decades of immersion in the subject, quite confident in saying that the historic experience of Jewish life in America deserves for the most part to be thought of as singular. Neither better nor worse, that history has in fact no parallel in modern Jewish history when it comes to the size of the Jewish population that formed there, the relative absence of encumbrances, and the creativity and improvisational flair of American

Jews as they felt empowered to remake Jewish tradition, as well as other matters that will become clearer in the chapters that follow in this book.

I do not imply here that only American Jews achieved political visibility, economic comfort, or institutional heft. Their coreligionists who immigrated to and lived in other places at the same time—England, Canada, and so on—did so as well. Until the rise of Nazism, the Jews of Germany had come to enjoy many of these benefits of modernity, as did those in France and other countries in western Europe. It is just that they did so more and more extensively in the United States because so many more of them chose to make their homes there and the conditions of communal and everyday life—the theme of this book—arrayed themselves in a particular way in America, not replicated elsewhere.

How America Met the Jews makes no pretense of being a point by point, detail by detail comparison between the historic experience of Jews in America and Jews in other places. When I write that Jews in America in the mid-nineteenth century began to impress themselves on the cityscapes of their chosen communities with magnificent synagogue buildings, I am not saying that they did not do so elsewhere. Rather, what I want to do here is to look at a place, the United States, that emerged as the most attractive destination for Jewish immigrants and explore why that was the case and what it meant for America and for the Jews.

This excursion across the full scope of American history, starting in the middle of the seventeenth century into the near present, through the lens of the Jews who migrated and settled there, throws light on such crucial and unresolved issues as race, religion, class, politics, and immigration, matters that shaped the nation and that persist into the twenty-first century. Jews had the experience they did in America because these five phenomena shaped its history and touched them profoundly.

This excursion, in order to protect myself here, must of necessity be general, verging possibly on the superficial. It does not follow a linear, chronological model, and in order to answer the big question that I have posed, I have had to glide over decades and centuries, moving back and forth across time. I realize that looking more closely and carefully at each one of these subjects in a systematic, chronological mode would have produced a more nuanced narrative, and each more nuanced narrative might have produced some very different answers to the big question.

It perhaps does not need to be said, but I will do so in any case, that when I refer to "American Jews" or "the Jews of the United States," or when I use other such totalizing formulations, including "Americans," I am fully aware of the tremendous variation, divisions, and differences of opinion that make the use of such expressions facile and generalizing. The divisions that sundered American society—geographic, ethnic, racial, class, religious and otherwise—provide the basic stuff of the nation's history. So too, southern and northern Jews differed not only from each other but among themselves, as did small town versus urban, Orthodox, nonreligious, Zionist, anti-Zionism, Conservative, Reform, poor and rich, and everything in between. Gender mattered tremendously, as did the proximity of individuals to the immigration experience. Arguing among themselves actually provides one of the overriding characteristics of this history, and the utter inability of this leader or that one to get the Jews of America to unite and figuratively speak with a single voice renders my invocation of "American Jews" problematic. In this book I aim though to isolate those behaviors and attitudes that seem most applicable and widespread, identifying differences when necessary.

In the main, however, *How America Met the* Jews takes as its subject America rather than the Jews. America, its history, stands here on center stage. American as a category of analysis also cannot be understood independently of the great diversity, divisions, and discord that pervaded the nation. I can be as much taken to task for using it as for referring to American Jews. But in using both I have aimed for something that comes close to approximating a recognizable common experience and identifying practices and attitudes that, as much as possible, transcended obvious and powerful differences.

Each one of the five chapters that follows could be a book in itself, or indeed each one could serve as the basis for a number of competing books that explore these matters more systematically, each arriving at competing conclusions.

But I offer this book in its present, generalizing, and nonchronological form in order to accomplish two ends, namely, to (happily) fulfill my obligation to the Department of Judaic Studies at Brown University and to launch a discussion that will transcend celebration and provide instead a new context for understanding the Jewish encounter with America.

Introduction

A Propitious Meeting

By the early twentieth century the United States became home to the largest Jewish enclave that ever existed, quite a demographic feat given the Jews' lengthy history, one that spanned millennia and took place on nearly the entirety of the globe. Never had so many Jews gathered within the borders of a single country or nation. A simple statement of fact based on empirical evidence, this numerical reality renders it worthy of thinking about in historical terms.

The project of thinking about it and trying to understand how it came to pass should not be construed as a value judgment or as a matter of declaring this a positive or negative development, although ultimately these perhaps cannot be avoided. Its size derived from a mammoth voluntary immigration, as Europe's Jews voted with their feet, leaving their home communities and making their way to America. The size of the Jewish population in America, its role as an immigrant destination, and its magnetic pull deserve to be explained in historical terms and in light of the question of what made America so attractive to them.

Jews settled in America and created there a population center that had in sheer numerical terms no rival among the many other lands where their forebears had once made their homes or where their contemporaries lived. Although heavily concentrated in a few large cities, with New York the behemoth among them, they also spread themselves across the land, settling in every region and state, creating a dazzling array of institutions and communal structures that reflected both their own expectations and the size of their communities, and were deeply impacted by American political, cultural, and economic realities.

Another constellation of numbers, whether evaluated as good or bad does not matter, tells a similar story. Over the course of the great century of migration, which extended from the 1820s through the 1920s, European Jews and indeed those from the Ottoman Empire who chose to leave the lands of their birth and residence and settled in some new nation state, opted for America more often than any other place. About one-third of world Jewry crossed some national boundary, assuming residence in some new land.

The United States emerged as the most sought after, most attractive destination in the world, unrivaled in terms of how many Jews wanted to go there as they made their way to a variety of new places of residence. More likely than not in that century, and indeed beyond, after global migrations stalled, almost any Jew in the world considering emigration put the United States at the top of her or his list of possible places to resume and rebuild life. Writing at the very start of the mass immigration to the United States, the German poet Heinrich Heine contrasted Jewish life in his homeland with that in America, where "a happier generation than ours blesses its palm branches and chews its unleavened bread by the Mississippi" River.[1]

The distinctiveness of America, when thought about in the context of the broad sweep of Jewish history, which played out over centuries, indeed millennia, and across continents, involved not just the size of its population but also a number of key characteristics that operated together to make the American Jewish experience notable.

The historian recognizes that every place she might choose to study can be described as "notable," as each city, region, or country had a distinctive history, each to be analyzed in terms of its particular spectrum of characteristics. The histories of all places pivoted around the specific experiences of the people who lived there, shaped by unique contingent forces. New York, Chicago, and Los Angeles may all be American cities, but each owed its origin to very different moments in time, attracted distinctive populations, developed its own economic bases, and each has to be seen as distinctive and notable. Belgium and the Netherlands may be geographically contiguous but they had different histories. So too Ireland and Scotland. Italy and Greece diverged and produced specific histories, both similar and dissimilar to each other.

Saying that the history of the Jews of the United States deserves to be thought of in its own context does not mean valorizing or disparaging it. Just the simple fact of the size of the Jewish population and America's overwhelming attractiveness as an immigration destination for Jews make it different from all other Jewish histories. The formative forces that shaped it, made it different from all the other centers of Jewish life, past and present, provide the basic theme of *How America Met the Jews*.

One example of that difference perhaps can be illustrative. From an internal Jewish perspective, America emerged as notable in global and historical terms in that no place else did Jewishness, however defined, constitute such a voluntary category. In few other places did the state allow such boundless latitude and exhibit such a lack of interest in how

---

1. Quoted in Albert M. Friedenberg, "A German Jewish Poet on America," *Publications of the American Jewish Historical Society* 13 (1905): 89–92.

Jews organized themselves into their communities. No rabbis operated with government sanction, no synagogues enjoyed official support, no institutions articulated positons that represented *the* voice of the Jewish community, and no Jewish schools received public monies, as happened in many other places. No chief rabbi presided over the Jews of the United States as did, for example, a continuous string of them in England, ever since 1704 when William II named Aaron Hart to this position, giving him the authority to govern the United Synagogues. Jews in France celebrated in 1831 when Judaism received official state recognition, putting it on an equal footing with Catholicism and Protestantism, and Jewish clergy, trained at an officially sponsored and tax-subsidized rabbinical seminary in the city of Metz, received their payment from state coffers. While this policy came to an end in 1905 when France secularized and stripped all religions of official status, no such interlude took place in America, where Jewish seminaries rose or fell, like those of other denominations, based on the support of their adherents. The state did not care who got trained where for what religious function or another, nor indeed who put the title "rabbi," "reverend," or "pastor" in front of their names. If enough people in a community considered these individuals worthy of clerical status, then, out of their own will, they deferred to these religious leaders, supported them, and gave them the honor that accompanied the position.

Jewish life in England and France may have most closely resembled that of America, but the presence of a chief rabbi in England and the Commonwealth or the power invested by the French government in the Israelite Central Consistory, convened in 1808 by Napoleon as *the* representative body of French Jewry, made these open and democratic societies different from America.

The high level of voluntarism that permeated American Jewish life meant that in America Jewish community never really existed other than as something imagined and invoked. No group, organization, or body could claim authority, and all such entities that did exist at one time or another bemoaned the absence of unity, the utter disarray of Jews, whether nationally or locally. Multiple organizations and institutions all claimed to speak for the Jews, but in reality each one spoke only for its members, the women and men who supported them with their dues and contributions, willingly donated. Each competed with all the others, often relying on the number of contributors and the size of their contributions as evidence of their importance. None could claim government authority.

The United States placed upon Jews few restrictions, and few disabling liabilities fettered them as they arrived, settled, and went about the business of creating the kinds of institutions they wanted, whether religious, social, cultural, or charitable. Certainly other new societies, particularly the settler societies that grew out of British colonization, such as

Canada and Australia, resembled the United States in this. But the vastly smaller number of Jews who lived in either place makes the comparisons somewhat beside the point, and those places also had Jewish histories of regulation and supervision by the various chief rabbis who, from London, maintained some authority over their flocks, the Jews who lived in the colonies and then the Commonwealth.

In the United States, as in those other places, Jews settled freely and established their enclaves, deciding as informally and voluntarily constituted communal bodies how to live and where, how to organize themselves, and how to interact with one another and their non-Jewish neighbors.

It is fair to say that they confronted in America more choices of how to express their Jewishness, how to define and fulfill their Jewish obligations, as well as where to build their homes, how to earn their bread, participate in civic life, and engage with their non-Jewish neighbors than most other Jews in the world.

This surely does not imply that they interacted seamlessly with America and that no clouds darkened an otherwise eternally sunny encounter. The history of their exclusions and limitations over the course of American history has been the subject of numerous scholarly studies. Those restrictions, whether in housing, jobs, admission to colleges and universities, and places of leisure, provided the motivation for Jewish communal leaders, all importantly self-appointed, to create many of their communal institutions and organizations, with the National Council of Jewish Women (1893), the American Jewish Committee (1905), and the Anti-Defamation League (1913) among the most enduring and visible.[2]

Jews in America, from their earliest days in the middle of the seventeenth century, recognized the animosities and suspicions with which some of their non-Jewish neighbors viewed them and smarted at the restrictions placed on them by the vastly larger Christian society, whether in terms of access to the schools they wanted to attend, jobs they hoped to secure, neighborhoods they wanted to live in, or hotels and resorts at which they desired to recreate. They found odious the dissemination of unpleasant images on stage, screen, and in print. When Jews in America saw words and deeds that they found offensive, they complained. They sought methods to combat such restrictions and organized themselves

---

2. Michael Dobkowski, *The Tarnished Dream: The Basis of American Anti-Semitism* (Westport, CT: Greenwood Press, 1979); Naomi W. Cohen, "Anti-Semitism in the Gilded Age: The Jewish View," *Jewish Social Studies* 41.3–4 (Summer/Fall 1979): 187–210; Leonard Dinnerstein, *Anti-Semitism in America* (Oxford: Oxford University Press, 1994). For more on Jewish defense organizations and their responses to anti-Semitism, see Stuart Svonkin, *Jews Against Prejudice: American Jews and the Fight for Civil Liberties* (New York: Columbia University Press, 1997).

communally when they believed that they had been denied what they wanted and deserved.[3]

But when looking at the broad arc of Jewish history and comparing it in terms of anti-Jewish practices and discourse, particularly in the many places where American Jews or their forebears had once lived, instances of what we might label here for the sake of convenience as anti-Semitism in the United States appear minimal and inconsequential. However much they smarted from these stings, however much Jews, at times, questioned their welcome in America, their leaders never encouraged them to move elsewhere, nor did the masses of them do so on their own. They recognized the problems arrayed against them in America but made no efforts to find some other, less hostile place.[4]

Our subjects, the Jews of America, consistently weighed the acts and instances of hostility amid which they lived in the United States against that which they had known "back home" in Germany, Poland, and the like, and for the most part considered the burdens they carried to be quite minimal. They approached American realities with a consciousness not only of what they or their parents had experienced in, say, Lithuania, Bavaria, or Ukraine, but they and the leaders of the community articulated a deep historic consciousness of Jewish persecution in the far past. In articles, sermons, fiction, and textbooks they referred to the horrors perpetrated against the Jews during the age of the Crusades, the massacres in Poland of the mid-seventeenth century, the expulsions from Spain, or England, and many others past acts of violence. These references stood in contrast to the relatively untroubled life they found in America.

So too Jews recognized the vast chasm between the difficulties they faced as opposed to those endured by so many other Americans, particularly those not defined as white, and that contrast resonated with them, as it should with us, as we think about the long history of America's encounter with the Jews. In the main, their multicentury experience in America, extending back to the seventeenth century and proceeding beyond, can be read as a narrative of fewer and weaker and ultimately nonexistent limitations, of so few moments of violence that they can be ticked off on the fingers of the hand.

Jews contemplating immigration to the United States had learned through multiple sources, including the Jewish press as well as letters from family and friends already living on the American side of the Atlantic, that in America Jews enjoyed privileges and had access to rights and

---

3. M. Alison Kibler, *Censoring Racial Ridicule: Irish, Jewish and African American Struggles over Race and Representation, 1890–1930* (Chapel Hill: University of North Carolina Press, 2015).

4. Tony Michels, "Is America "Different"? A Critique of American Jewish Exceptionalism, " *American Jewish History* 96.3 (2010): 201–224.

opportunities denied to many other Americans. In America they could count themselves on the better side of many deeply embedded divides in the society based on class, ethnicity, religion, and most importantly color. In a novel moment in their long history of being the hated other, defined as such by the countries where they lived, those who made the move across the ocean to America arrived entitled rather than disabled. Those entitlements spared them not only ghettoes, massacres, and a maze of restrictive legislation but also the constant understanding, built into their basic communal and personal lives, that they could not *ipso facto* assume the rights of full citizenship.

Many among the traditionalists in Europe and even some of those who themselves came to America viewed this unfolding of opportunities and expansion of freedoms for Jews with a degree of trepidation, fearing that the lack of meaningful barriers would be the death knell of communal solidarity. Rabbis in parts of eastern Europe counseled against the migration, warning that too warm a welcome awaited the Jews, who would because of that abandon commitment to tradition. The internal Jewish critics of America considered that America greeted the Jews just a bit too warmly, somewhat too easily, and that Jewish solidarity and cohesion could not withstand the opportunities. By the early twentieth century, advocates for a Jewish homeland in Palestine, the Zionists, also warned that America offered too many options and that such an elaborate set of American possibilities would lead to the loss of Jewish integrity and authenticity. They advocated instead for a Jewish homeland, based on a revived Jewish language, Hebrew. They envisioned an eventual Jewish majority, the flowering of, as they claimed, authentic Jewish cultural forms, unpolluted by the almost promiscuous hybridization taking place in America. By embracing such a future they hoped to avoid the messy encounters between the Jews and America, which, as they saw it, fostered too much Jewish integration with others, and therefore threatened the fraying of group ties. America, proponents of religious traditionalism and Jewish nationalism warned the Jews, would metaphorically love you to death.

But in articulating their fears as they did, the religiously observant, some of whom while still living in Europe, as well as Zionists, pointed to a reality worth thinking of in historical terms. They recognized the breadth of possibilities Jews in the United States enjoyed and the degree to which American realities, whether cultural, economic, social, or political, offered a kind of symbolic welcome mat to the Jews. Those options included wide-open participation in civic life, with as large a bundle of rights as available to anyone, success in the marketplace, the ability to move around as they desired, the crafting of practices and identities of their choice, and winning for their religious tradition a place of respect in the public consciousness.

How and why this history developed as it did provides the key question for this book. This question has never been asked quite like this. Certainly many books and articles, lectures, symposia, and courses have charted the history of the Jews in the United States.[5] The subject of American Jewish history has been discussed in a focused manner since the 1890s with the founding of the American Jewish Historical Society, which in its publications and scholarly journal has sought to describe and analyze the contours of this experience. Efforts to understand what is sometimes referred to as "the" American Jewish experience continued into the twentieth century, as scholars and communal leaders considered it imperative to tell their story to themselves, their children, and their American neighbors, both the broad public and public officials.

During the year 1954 and then fifty years later, in 2004–2005, as American Jewry marked the 300th and 350th year of Jewish life in America, harkening back to the arrival of the first twenty-three Jews to New Amsterdam, a flurry of public events and discussions, publications and programs embarked on the narration of this history. The producers of museum exhibitions, television programs, and pedagogic materials considered it important that Jews and non-Jews in America know about the history of the Jews among them. Their reasons have been complex, politically driven, and reflect the shifting historical moments when Jews in America took upon themselves the project of detailing the facts and sketching out the themes of their American years.[6]

But in the main, these historical re-creations and recitations focused on what the Jews did and said, what they accomplished and contributed, drawing attention to the Jews as the authors, as it were, of their own destiny. These projects of historical reclamation have primarily reflected what Jews thought about their own collective actions over time. For the most part, with certain notable exceptions, much of this history has emphasized the point that Jews, with their commitment to family, education, and hard work, ably navigated circumstances in their new home. The presentations, whether directed at Jewish audiences alone or to the broader public, trained their lenses on the Jews themselves.

The presenters of American Jewish history have chronicled the lives

5. Synthetic histories of the American Jewish experience include Hasia Diner, *The Jews of the United States, 1654–2000* (Berkeley: University of California Press, 2004); Jonathan Sarna, *American Judaism: A History* (New Haven: Yale University Press, 2004); Henry Feingold, ed., *The Jewish People in America*, 6 vols. (Baltimore, MD: Johns Hopkins University Press, 1992); Gerald Sorin, *Tradition Transformed: The Jewish Experience in America* (Baltimore, MD: Johns Hopkins University Press, 1997); Abraham Karp, *Haven and Home: A History of the Jews in America* (New York: Schocken Books, 1985); and Arthur Hertzberg, *The Jews in America: Four Centuries of an Uneasy Encounter. A History* (New York: Columbia University Press, 1997).
6. Beth Wenger, *History Lessons: The Creation of American Jewish Heritage* (Princeton, NJ: Princeton University Press, 2010).

and contributions of individual Jews who helped make America, serving the common good. Whether reciting the deeds of important individuals—soldiers and statesmen, social reformers or philanthropists, composers, writers, scientists, and artists—or if they detailed the collective actions of "the Jews," in a particular city, region, or the nation as a whole, they put American Jews on center stage. The historical narrative, as told to general and scholarly audiences, put much emphasis on how Jews banded together to work for themselves, for the Jewish people around the world, and for the benefit of America.

The story as told emphasized how Jews, as permanent immigrants to the United States, had few options but to find ways to succeed, and most did. By doing so, they contributed to American political life, its popular culture, and the nation's intellectual, social, and cultural work, making America a better place than they found it.

Some of these renditions of the American Jewish past, like the bold state-of-the art National Museum of American Jewish History in Philadelphia, situated on no less sacred a space than Independence Mall, which opened in 2010, did bring America into the narrative. The museum planners did so in the main as celebrations of the nation and its ethos of freedom.

The word "freedom" resonated deeply in the telling of American Jewish history. Oscar Handlin, one of the nation's most distinguished historians and indeed the first Jew to get tenure in Harvard University's prestigious history department, wrote *Adventure in Freedom* (1954), one of the earliest overviews of that history, using the singular "adventure" to imply that there had been one and only one like it.[7] More than sixty years later, the Philadelphia museum continued that descant. On every floor, as museum goers learn the story of the American Jews, they take a journey from "Foundations of Freedom" to "Dreams of Freedom" to "Choices and Challenges of Freedom," reaching the narrative's culmination on the ground floor with an "American Jewish Hall of Fame," graced with the aphorism "Only in America," and as such conjoining the valorization of Jews of achievement and the ecstatic celebration of America as the embodiment of something called "freedom."

How America Met the Jews narrates this history from a different angle, avoiding the unquestioned and indeed bombastic use of the word "freedom." This book seeks to provide in a more fully developed and critical manner an analysis that avoids rhetoric and jingoism, that eschews celebrations of Jews or America, but rather asks, as the title states, how did America meet the Jews? That is, it takes as its project the matter of how some of the most profound aspects of American history and culture cre-

---

7. Oscar Handlin, *Adventure in Freedom* (New York: McGraw-Hill, 1954).

ated for the Jews, from the eighteenth century onward, to be a bit trite for a moment, something of a "promised land." How can we explain the almost magnetic attraction that America had for the Jews, particularly those who in the long nineteenth century realized that they had to leave their places of residence and weighed and measured the range of places where they could go? Why America, beyond the fact that as increasing numbers of Jews did go to America, more and more Jews in villages and towns in Alsace, Bohemia, Lithuania, Ukraine, and various spots in the Ottoman Empire then had friends and family already in New York, Chicago, San Francisco, or the Mississippi Delta? What aspects of America pulled them in, as their familiar homes pushed them out? What *was* the United States for them—quite a tall order here—and how did key characteristics of its political, social, and economic life offer them a setting so attractive that the country served as both a giant magnet and an incubator for Jewish personal and communal development?

Obviously the concept of a "promised land" does not assume any kind of divine unfolding of this history or conflate the migration to America with some kind of biblical mission, growing out of Jewish scripture.[8] Yet American rabbis and Jewish community leaders since the middle of the nineteenth century, as well as the writers of patriotic and celebratory works for Jewish children, tried to make the point that American and Jewish "values" dovetailed so perfectly that an almost divine plan must have been at work, that an otherworldly pre-ordained script must have somehow been there, inspiring so many Jews to opt for the United States. They pointed to the fact that Puritans of New England, those who according to one rendition of American history shaped the nation that would emerge as the United States, referred to themselves as the "new Israelites," who described their flight from England in the terms of the Hebrews' exodus from Egyptian slavery, that they bestowed upon their children names drawn from the Hebrew Bible and dotted Massachusetts and Connecticut with names like Canaan, Sharon, Goshen, Hebron, Salem, and the like. Celebrants of the American–Jewish synthesis loved to point out that the patriots emblazoned the Liberty Bell with words from Leviticus ("And proclaim liberty throughout the land") and that the most American of holidays, Thanksgiving, took as its model and inspiration, as described by

---

8. In my own scholarship, I have relied on promised-land terminology, and I did so not ironically. My first book, *In the Almost Promised Land: American Jews and Blacks, 1915–1935*, examined how Jews made sense of America's racial realities. My later book, *A New Promised Land: A History of Jews in America*, was a volume I contributed to the Oxford University Press's library on American religions for young readers. See Hasia Diner, *In the Almost Promised Land: American Jews and Blacks, 1915–1935* (Baltimore, MD: Johns Hopkins University Press, 1995); Hasia Diner, *A New Promised Land: A History of Jews in America* (Oxford: Oxford University Press, 2003).

William Bradford, the governor of the Plymouth colony, the Jews' harvest festival of Sukkot.

Surely, so many Jewish commentators declared, whether out of sincere belief or for political purposes, the history of the Jews in America and the history of America must reflect some deeply intertwined bond, transcendent in origins. They have argued that, in the words of one rabbi, Stuart Gordon, *America Is Different.*[9]

Early twentieth-century American Jewish flirtations with the Columbus story tried to make that point as well, speculating that perhaps something more than random coincidence had been at work when in 1492, the worst year in Jewish history to that point, the time when the wrenching, cataclysmic expulsion of the Jews from Spain transpired, Columbus, the navigator from Genoa, persuaded the Jews' great enemy, Queen Isabella, to permit him to sail westward. In the process he "discovered" America, their eventual place of refuge. American Jewish communal notables, some deeply involved with the American Jewish Historical Society, tinkered with the idea that Columbus had been a Jew and that his voyages to Europe's new world could rightly be seen as an effort to scout out a better place for his people. Was not the country that would emerge from the Columbian voyage a fulfillment of biblical prophecy? All of this, some speculated, constituted hints and clues about America's singularity for the Jews, that its founding and development constituted elements of a nearly messianic drama, making it unlike any other country, one to be seen as more than just another large diaspora home.[10]

In a similar, although somewhat less fanciful vein, scholars and American Jewish communal leaders sought to discover the affinity between Judaism and democracy, and particularly between Jewish tradition and America's brand of democracy. Milton Konvitz, son of a rabbi, born in Palestine, came to America in 1915. A prolific scholar, an engaged and active liberal, he wrote broadly on the U.S. Constitution, human rights, American political thought, and the like. In his lengthy bibliography appear such titles as *Judaism and Human Rights, Judaism and the American Idea,* and *Torah and Constitution,* all offering trenchant arguments as to why Jewish tradition and American ideals of progress, democracy, and freedom dovetail with each other and how the latter helped shape the former.[11]

---

9. Michael Hoberman, *New Israel/New England: Jews and Puritans in Early America* (Amherst: University of Massachusetts Press, 2011); Stuart E. Gordon, *America Is Different: The Search for Jewish Identity* (New York: T. Nelson, 1964).

10. Meyer Kayserling, *Christopher Columbus and the Participation of Jews in the Spanish and Portuguese Discoveries* (New York: Longmans and Green, 1928); Simon Wiesenthal, *Sails of Hope: The Secret Mission of Christopher Columbus* (New York: Macmillan, 1973).

11. Milton Konvitz, ed., *Judaism and Human Rights* (Livingston, NJ: Transaction Publishers, 2001); Milton Konvitz, *Judaism and the American Idea* (New York: Schocken Books,

How America Met the Jews moves in a much more prosaic direction, discerning no divine promises, seeking no evidence of the workings of providence. Rather it wants to offer an analysis of how and why the United States emerged as the most-sought-after destination for Jews, individuals and families, in the great age of migration and beyond. It charts out how the particularities of American life, not the vaunted and unexamined "freedom" of Oscar Handlin's adventure or the narrative of the National Museum of American Jewish History, made possible the creation of distinctively American Jewish history, how the emergence of distinctively American social, political, and economic patterns of life enhanced the attractiveness of the United States for Jews.

Without engaging in hyperbole, It can be said and proven that American realities made it possible for Jews, as individuals, men for most of that history, and women eventually, to have a robust range of options in the public sphere, as one by one they entered into the marketplace and the voting booth, as they went out on the roads, into classrooms, and workspaces, unencumbered by the fact of their Jewishness.

That last statement could also describe other places as well in the modern era, but more Jews had this experience in America because more of them lived there. So too, America made possible and its Jews created there the largest, most elaborately organized, most well-endowed, least-encumbered, institutionally plastic and culturally pluralistic Jewish community in the world, possibly in all of Jewish history.

The nature of American life, its economic, political, racial, demographic, and religious realities, evolved over time and provide a set of explanatory contexts or factors by which to think about what happened and why for the Jews. Those realities all grew together out of the soil of American history and their convergence should be seen as historically contingent.

All of these factors, to some degree, existed, in some cases in protean fashion, since the seventeenth century when the first Jews arrived in the North American colonies of Britain and the Netherlands, but their growth and flowering over time, coinciding with the great push of the Jews out of Europe, created a kind of alchemy that in turn produced an environment that "worked" for the Jews.

Each one of these factors, five of them, and their synergistic interaction with each other helps describe and analyze the basic question here of how America met the Jews. These themes include (1) the centrality and nature of immigration to America, (2) the nation's enduring obsession with color, (3) American materialism, linked to its economic dynamism, (4) the religious landscape, which by default and design fostered the existence of multiple

---

1980); Milton Konvitz, *Torah and Constitution: Essays in American Jewish Thought* (Syracuse, NY: Syracuse University Press, 1998).

denominations, and (5) the relatively nonideological structure of America's political life, with its long-standing commitment to just two parties.

Each of these matters will constitute a chapter in this book, and each chapter will describe these realities and explore how they acted upon the Jews, benefited them, and how they, the Jews, took advantage of them. As such, this book offers itself as more of a discourse on American history than on Jewish history. But it assumes that anyone interested in American Jewish history has to take seriously the particular structure of the American setting, not as background but as fundamental to what happened to the Jews who moved there.

The focus on the American context as formative and the statement that the history of the Jews who settled within its borders cannot be understood without a deep immersion into American history do not imply that Jews passively accepted what they found, that they did not influence its developments. The Jews in America, even before national independence, played a role in pushing forward those elements in American life that they believed advantaged them and in weakening those elements that held them back or disadvantaged them. But still the Jews functioned over the course of that history as the beneficiaries rather than as the prime actors. Their small numbers made that inevitable as did the fundamentally Protestant nature of civic life, the commitment of the larger society to Americanization, a process that some consider tantamount to homogenization, and the strong pressure toward cultural conformity.

A few words are in order in terms of the basic arc of the history of the Jews as their experience coincided with that of America. This history began in the seventeenth century. The year 1654 is the usual date given for when the first group of Jews, as opposed to lone individuals, showed up in New Amsterdam—a contingent of Atlantic world people, whose presence in the Western Hemisphere reflected the European penetration of a world not theirs.[12] From the end of the seventeenth century and through the eighteenth, Jews functioned in British North America as a numerically insignificant portion of the population who interacted with the larger American society devoid of any assumed entitlements, although those entitlements grew with few serious and enflamed public discussions of their worthiness or lack thereof. Over the course of the next two centuries, starting in the 1820s with the beginnings of Jewish mass migration and the dawn of the "age of the common man," which removed property qualifications from white male voting and the last vestiges of state religious

---

12. Holly Snyder has questioned the 1654 "beginnings" of the American Jewish experience in Holly Snyder, "Rethinking the Definition of 'Community' in a Migratory Age, 1654–1830," in *Imagining the American Jewish Community*, ed. Jack Wertheimer (Hanover, NH: University Press of New England/Brandeis University Press, 2007), 3–27.

establishments, Jews arrived at a point in their history where they could claim utter privilege, chained down by no fetters as they enjoyed access to every aspect of American citizenship.[13]

In that process Jewish women and men of America proceeded from a situation in which they affirmatively sought anonymity as Jews, occupying in their early history literally unmarked Jewish spaces. The structural environment in fact offers a good example of change over time, of how the Jews of America increasingly claimed visibility for themselves. Not until the 1850s, for example, did they build synagogues upon which they marked words, symbols, and motifs that denoted that Jews occupied these spaces. Until then they hid behind unassuming exteriors, worshiping in structures that lacked on the outside any Jewish specificity. By the decade before the Civil War they began to assert themselves, feeling able and eager to boldly put their particular stamp on the American landscape. Over time their buildings proliferated, becoming larger and more prominently placed in the most prestigious spots in any town or city. In the decades after the 1860s they commissioned ornate, lofty synagogues, designed in the Moorish style, an architectural choice that had no Christian equivalents; and in this Jews in America willingly pointed to their distinctiveness.

This striving for visibility only increased over the course of the twentieth century. Three buildings deserve quick mention to demonstrate the degree to which American Jews came to assert themselves into and onto the nation's structural environment. In 1993 the Holocaust Memorial Museum opened its doors on the National Mall, in close proximity to those shrines of American nationalism, the Lincoln and Washington Memorials. While not officially a Jewish communal structure, the Holocaust Museum grew out of American Jewish political concerns, raising much of its funding from American Jews; in the main it tells a very Jewish story, and one that emphasizes the beneficence of America by its absence from the horrendous narrative. So too the Museum of Jewish Heritage in New York, inaugurated in 1997, looks out on two of the most iconic symbols of American history, the Statue of Liberty and Ellis Island, two national structures that Jews have claimed to be central to their narrative as well. The National Museum of American Jewish History also provides a case in point, in that Jews claimed a spot on the holy swathe of land in Philadelphia flanked by Independence Hall, the Liberty Bell, and the National Constitution Center. Indeed no other religious or ethnic community has planted itself so centrally and frontally in the American national landscape.

---

13. For two books that attempted to tell the entirety of that story, see Diner, *Jews of the United States*, and Sarna, *American Judaism*. Both books appeared, independent of each other, simultaneously with the 350th anniversary.

The opening in 2004 of the Smithsonian Institution's Museum of the American Indian and the launch of the African American Museum in 2016 do not contradict the statement that Jews have been unique in America as a religious or ethnic community for the kind of public attention they have received in the public sphere. The two museums, the one for the extirpated, raped, and robbed indigenous people and the other for the descendants of the involuntarily transferred and enslaved millions of Africans can be thought of as statements of moral obligation by the nation to those it harmed most grievously. But no other religious community or any other group whose ancestors voluntarily chose to immigrate to America has planted itself as prominently on America's civic space as the Jews.

Yet over the course of their history, Jewish women and men of America, who once worshiped in buildings undistinguished by Hebrew words, the Ten Commandments, Stars of David, the twelve tribes of Israel, or lions of Judah on their exterior walls, by the end of the twentieth century built themselves centrally into the nation's sacred narrative, putting themselves, as Jews, into its physical spaces.

So too, the trajectory of that history involved a movement by which they, a small band who in September 1654 had to beg Peter Stuyvesant, the governor general of New Amsterdam, to allow them to stay, and willingly accepted the limitations he placed on them, increasingly felt comfortable and empowered to make their case, or cases, in their own name and to state that despite their integration into America, they had a distinctive political agenda, shaped by their Jewishness. They began their communal lives in the new United States also a bit skittish, not sure as to where exactly they would fit in and what status they would occupy, nervous even after the adoption of the Constitution, which made it clear that in the political realm at least, religion and nativity would handicap no one.

Members of several of the Jewish congregations, the ones in Savannah, Georgia, and Newport, Rhode Island, communicated with George Washington just as he was about to assume his presidency. For centuries American Jews pointed with pride to the fact that he answered them at all and promised that the nation at whose helm he now stood would offer "to bigotry no sanction," as he wished well for those of the "stock of Abraham." In 1946, with the ashes of the destroyed Jewry of Europe still smoldering, the Newport congregation's home, the 1763 Touro Synagogue, won designation as a National Historic Site, administered by the United States government. While that decision had a complex history independent of the Holocaust, for American Jewry it served as a statement of what American meant for them and how their history deviated so profoundly from that of their kin who had not traveled across the Atlantic, whether by sail or steam power. So too they pointed out with pride that the nation that had welcomed them, that had promised "to bigotry no sanction," recognized the deep connection between their two histories.[14]

At some point in their history, the Jews of the United States moved beyond doubt and began to feel able to state that when it came to the great public issues of the day, they as Jews had their own, group-specific stake in the outcome. Over time, for example, Jews, as demonstrated by the words and actions of their organizations, organs of public opinion, and networks of communication, moved from quietly asking the vastly larger Christian society to give to Judaism some of the same privileges that the Protestant denominations enjoyed to eventually standing up and demanding not only equal rights for Jews and Judaism but pushing American society to change itself. From a population that had pleaded, somewhat meekly, that Judaism be considered a legitimate American faith community, Jews ultimately perceived themselves as able and empowered to take on America and demand that some of the nation's most fundamental institutions and practices change.

Three examples should suffice here. By the late nineteenth century many American Jews began to chide America for its deep commitment to the idea of laissez-faire as the best way to structure relations between the classes. Many American Jews, including the leaders of some of the most prestigious bodies, such as the Reform movement through its Union of American Hebrew Congregations, came to demand that the state enter into the economic life of the nation not as an advocate for business but as an advocate for workers and for the poor.[15] So too, by the early twentieth century nearly all American Jewish organs of public opinion, in English and Yiddish, joined in a pioneering assault on American race relations, lambasting the United States for the pervasiveness of racism and calling

14. Esther Schwartz, *Restoration of the Touro Synagogue* (Newport, RI: Rhode Island Jewish Historical Society, 1959). More information on the history of the Touro Synagogue and the exchange between colonial Jews and George Washington can be found in a number of volumes including George Goodwin and Ellen Smith, eds., *The Jews of Rhode Island* (Hanover, NH: University Press of New England/Brandeis University Press, 2004).

15. For Jews and the New Deal, see Leonard Dinnerstein, "Jews and the New Deal," *American Jewish History* 72.4 (1983): 461–76. For a small representation of books about American Jewish support for the labor movement, see Tony Michels, *A Fire in Their Hearts: Yiddish Socialists in New York* (Cambridge, MA: Harvard University Press, 2005); Paula Hyman, "Immigrant Women and Consumer Protest: The New York Kosher Meat Boycott of 1902," *American Jewish History* 70.1 (1982): 91–105; and Alice Kessler Harris, "Organizing the Unorganizable: Three Jewish Women and Their Union," *Labor History* 17 (1976): 5–23. The history of American Jewish liberalism can be found in Marc Dollinger, *The Quest for Inclusion: Jews and Liberalism in Modern America* (Princeton, NJ: Princeton University Press, 2000); and Arthur Goren, *The Politics and Public Culture of American Jews* (Bloomington: Indiana University Press, 1999). Michael Staub offers a critique of a singular American Jewish liberalism in the pre–World War II period in Michael Staub, *Torn at the Roots: The Crisis of Jewish Liberalism in Postwar America* (New York: Columbia University Press, 2002).

on Americans to fully live up to the nation's rhetorical creed of equality. Despite the deeply entrenched culture of white racism, which benefited the Jews, individual Jews from the beginning of the century and, by the 1930s and 1940s, Jewish organizations joined African Americans and white liberals in a fight against the racial hierarchy, a system so intricately woven into the fabric of American life.[16] Finally, beginning in the latter part of the nineteenth century and then even more forcefully after World War II Jews willingly stood out and apart from the many times larger Christian population in their critique of the persistence of cracks in the wall between church and state. This willingness to challenge Christian, largely Protestant, hegemony had roots in Jewish political action, commencing in the mid-nineteenth century and reaching its zenith after World War II,as Jews told the overwhelmingly Christian population of the United States that they did not in fact have the right to claim America as a Christian nation.[17]

This book will not treat in any extended manner the internal changes within American Jewry particularly vis-à-vis the practice of Judaism. It will, however, look at the impact of American ideas about religion and how they played a crucial role in shaping the ways by which Jewish people in America came to define and redefine Judaism and the nature of Jewish life as a malleable entity, as something that they usually quite ordinary and unlettered women and men, could mold to fit their various beliefs, sensibilities, and tastes. Over such deeply significant issues of language, ritual, and communal governance, American Jews in their local communities, more intensely and more often than their sisters and brothers elsewhere, created religious practices and institutions that worked for them, confirming the words of Rabbi Mordecai Kaplan that Jewish law had only a "vote" but no "veto" power.

No issue has been more central to this than that of gender and women's rights. In America, and to echo the hackneyed phrase "only in America," did Jewish women move from behind the curtains of public invisibility to the center stage of the leadership of Judaism, demanding and winning the right to be voting members of synagogues and serve as rabbis and cantors, religious positions for millennia occupied only by men. American realities made it possible for Jewish women to find ways to give themselves voice and challenge the male leadership of their community to decouple religious responsibilities and rights from gender. Jewish women in no other country asserted as did those in America that they should literally count and that when it came to participating in public manifestations of Judaism. Only these Jewish women, shaped by

16. Diner, *In the Almost Promised Land*; Cheryl Greenberg, *Troubling the Waters: Black-Jewish Relations in the American Century* (Princeton, NJ: Princeton University Press, 2006).

17. Kevin Schultz, *Tri-Faith America: How Catholics and Jews Held Postwar America to Its Protestant Promise* (Oxford: Oxford University Press, 2011).

American realities, argued as vociferously and successfully that even — or particularly — in the sacred spheres of synagogue and seminary, biology ought not be anyone's destiny.[18]

Much of this may smack of the much maligned, and deservedly so, paradigm of American exceptionalism, a discarded mode of thinking and doing history that assumed that America had a history unlike that of so many other places in the world, and that history ought to be read as positive and progressive. In general in the field of American history, the old idea of exceptionalism has in fact been thoroughly replaced by a much more nuanced, perhaps negative, view, informed in part by comparative research, the emergence of global thinking, and the elevation of thinking about race as a key aspect of American life. American exceptionalism, certainly when it involved holding up America as more democratic, more humane, as more progressive and more advanced, as a mode of writing and thinking about the past withered in the face of both transnational analysis and the voluminous studies of the last decades concerned with slavery, racism, the eradication of native peoples, and armed aggression against small nations, among other subjects. As involving some of those, indeed America may have been exceptional in the scale of its brutality and the extent of its harshness rather than its beneficence.

But in the case of Jewish history, the reality of exceptionalism still holds forth and with some justification. It conforms to a long-held view in the field of Jewish history that America and the history of its Jews stood in a class by itself. In the academy only American Jewish history is thought of as a field separate from modern Jewish history. While obviously some historians specialize in German Jewish history, Polish Jewish history, French Jewish history, and the like, only American Jewish historians have the full apparatus of a separate field, with journals, a scholarly society, two large archives with the word "American" in their titles, and a biennial conference of their own. Courses in "modern Jewish history" generally do not include America but take Europe, and increasingly the Ottoman Empire and North Africa, as the geographic focus.

The rationale behind this organization of knowledge assumes, probably rightly, that not only did American Jews have a different history from most other Jews in the world but that this history embodied the idea and essence of modernity. This, for the most part, has not caused any distancing or strain between them and the historians of Jewish life in other places, some of whom have also begun to find ways to incorporate American themes into their work.

American Jewish historians write and conceptualize their field in a way

---

18. Karla Goldman, *Beyond the Synagogue Gallery: Finding a Place for Women in American Judaism* (Cambridge, MA: Harvard University Press, 2001); Pam Nadell, *Women Who Would Become Rabbis: A History of Women's Ordination, 1889–1985* (Boston: Beacon Press, 1999).

that betokens something of the aura of exceptionalism, and in a positive sense, and that may explain why something of a gap exists between them and other Americanists who rightly over the last few decades have been engaged in a project of dismantling the very idea that the story of American history involved a narrative of progress, the expansion of rights, and the flowering of opportunities, whether economic, political, or cultural.

That gap may not be reconcilable. After all, from the perspective of Jewish history, it has been a history of progress, expansion of rights, and the flowering of opportunities. The history of American Jewry has been largely built around the fact of the absence of a demonstrable and clear process of legal emancipation. American Jewry never went through this excruciating and excruciatingly long ordeal. For certain in the seventeenth and eighteenth centuries different colonies maintained different policies vis-à-vis Jewish settlement and Jewish political rights; these restrictions represented the carry-over of English policies. Similarly in those British colonies Jews suffered no more handicaps than other religious minority groups, Catholics in particular, who indeed suffered much more. In the early republic, three of the original thirteen, Maryland, New Hampshire, and North Carolina, continued, each differently, to maintain restrictions on Jewish officeholding, but notably these states did not limit these restrictions to Jews but also to men who belonged to a number of outsider religious communities and to "nonbelievers," the great scourge of the deeply religious Protestant majority. These restrictions impacted only a relatively small number of individual Jewish men in Maryland, since a fully formed community had not yet congealed there, while in the other two states restrictions on Jewish officeholding functioned as a matter of rhetoric rather than a real policy that sought to exclude actual people. For most of that history, no Jews lived in either place, rendering the restrictions abstract and fictive rather than punishing and hurtful. All of these vestiges of the prenational period came to an end in 1824 in Maryland, and in the other two states in the 1860s and 1870s with the passage and implementation of the Fourteenth Amendment.[19]

More importantly, no state admitted after the creation of the United States, the other thirty-seven, maintained any legal restrictions on Jewish participation. Indeed one of the first acts of the newly formed Congress after the revolution, the Northwest Ordinance of 1787, which set the terms by which newly acquired lands could become official territories and then eventually seek statehood, expressly guaranteed untrammeled religious freedom.

This history stands in stark contrast to the history of the legalized oth-

---

19. Morton Borden, *Jews, Turks, and Infidels* (Chapel Hill: University of North Carolina Press, 2011), 38. New Hampshire removed its restriction of Catholic and Jewish officeholding in 1877.

ering of Jews every place else in the "old" world, where Jews in one place after another lived. England, France, the Austro-Hungarian Empire, Germany, Italy, and Russia all had long histories that involved Jews living as a separate class, at times tolerated, at other times expelled, and long drawn-out journeys toward emancipation. In each one of those places the halls of national and regional governments echoed with debates over the worthiness, or lack thereof, of the Jews for inclusion into the nation.

In each one of those countries, over lengthy periods of time, notable non-Jewish individuals banded together and tried to convince their fellow lawmakers and others with power that the Jews deserved some or all rights and that if the Jews did become emancipated, they would cease behaving in their traditionally obnoxious Jewish ways. The history of the United States offers us only one such small story. Thomas Kennedy, a representative in the Maryland General Assembly in the 1820s, sponsored the "Jew Bill," which passed after several failed attempts on his part to get it through the legislature. He argued with his fellow assemblymen not that the Jews would improve their character if they could finally hold office, the only restriction that the state's Test Act imposed upon them. Instead he declared that even though in "Maryland there are very few" Jews, "but if there was only one—to that one, we ought to do justice."[20]

American Jewish history has furthermore been defined as different from other Jewish histories in large measure because the kind of anti-Jewish behavior that took place in the United States, as opposed to in other places, has been understood in the context of the legacies of ghettoes, pogroms, expulsions, and ultimately the Holocaust. Accurately or not, much of the history of the Jews of Europe, England obviously excepted, has been cast in teleological terms. Historians writing the histories of those other Jewish communities knew their outcomes, the vast slaughter of the Jews, perpetrated not only by Germans but abetted in many places by the French, Polish, Dutch, Belgian, Italian, and so on, neighbors of the Jews.

A question that at times ripples through American Jewish discourse asks if it could have happened here and if, for example, had Germany in World War II invaded the United States, how would Americans have responded to the plight of their Jewish neighbors. Such flights of fantasy remain matters of speculation and projection, the stuff of novels, like Philip Roth's *The Plot Against America* (2004), which fancifully imagined a counterhistory to the one that actually transpired.

But it did not happen, and neither did explosions of mass violence or state-mandated badges or identity cards with the word "Jew" stamped on them. Jews like other white Americans never experienced forced residen-

---

20. Edward Eitches, "Maryland's Jew Bill," *American Jewish Historical Quarterly* 60 (1971), 258–78.

tial segregation. At no time did Jews get driven from their homes, leaving behind few traces of their lives once lived there.[21]

The absence of meaningful state-generated discrimination has made the narrative of the American Jewish experience not only a basically upbeat one but has also pushed historians to think about it in its own terms and not as part of the larger narrative of modern Jewish history. The anti-Jewish practices that proliferated, and they did, particularly from the 1920s into the postwar period, losing steam after the late 1940s and particularly the 1960s, emanated from private sources.

The slings and arrows hurt, yet the Jews, the women and men who found themselves at the short end of the benefits society offered, had no need to blame the government, its elected officials, its civil servants, and its basic institutions and documents.

How America Met the Jews hopes to avoid the twin trap of fileopietism and whiggishness, the former praising the Jews for the sterling traits that facilitated their success and the latter assuming that an inevitable path toward progress unfolded as the Jews arrived in small and then larger number as immigrants to America. Rather it operates on the knowledge that American realities helped to create and provided the environment that grew over time and had a history best analyzed in analytic categories different and apart from the experiences of other Jewish peoples, and that America—the United States—played a key role in making that singularity possible.

The five overarching realities of American life, present in one form or another from the seventeenth century onward, but increasing in prominence and intensity by the middle of nineteenth, including immigration, the color question, economic expansion, religious pluralism, and two-party politics stripped of any ideology besides the support of capitalism, provided the basic soil in which American Jewish communal life could take root and flourish, making it a, indeed the, most attractive destination for emigrating European Jews. These five, not present together in any other place in a similar way, helped foster the Jews' accelerating integration, even in periods when social discrimination pervaded much of American life. Each one of these existed as a separate element on the American scene but operated in conjunction with the others. Their confluence functioned as the matrix around which this history played itself out. While one cannot say with certainty that if any of these had not been present the history of the Jews would have taken a different course, but there is no need to speculate. They all existed. They influenced each other, and they all provided the basic outline of American history; and, overlaid one upon the other, they pivoted around each other and beckoned Europe's Jews, greeting them upon their arrival and structuring their American lives.

---

21. Phillip Roth, *The Plot Against America* (New York: Houghton-Mifflin, 2004).

1

Jewish Newcomers in a Nation of (White) Immigrants

Walt Whitman in his 1855 *Leaves of Grass* described the United States in lyrical terms, declaiming, "These states are the amplest poem/Here is not merely a nation but a teeming Nation of nations."[1] John F. Kennedy, slightly more than a century later, quoted Whitman as he sought to secure the Democratic Party's nomination for the presidency in 1960. The Massachusetts senator, only the second Catholic to run for the presidency and himself the grandson of immigrants from Ireland, authored a little book in 1958 at the behest of one of America's oldest Jewish defense organizations, the Anti-Defamation League of the B'nai B'rith, entitled fittingly *A Nation of Immigrants*. In the book, actually written by Harvard historian Oscar Handlin, the soon-to-be elected Kennedy called for the reform of the nation's immigration laws, which had been forged in the 1920s. Kennedy highlighted Whitman's invocation of immigration from abroad as one, indeed possibly the, force that gave the United States its distinctive nature.

Whitman's verse echoed beyond Kennedy's book, and the theme, articulated in many rhetorical variations, has continued to be invoked by commentators of all sorts in the half century since its publication and the passage in 1965 of the Hart-Cellar Act, which wiped out the national-origins quota system. Exemplified most dramatically in the Smithsonian National Museum of American History, with its grand Nation of Nations exhibit, first mounted on the occasion of the bicentennial, this verse offers a powerful way to think about immigration to the United States as a determining phenomenon for the course of Jewish history.[2]

Between the time of Whitman and that of Kennedy and Hart-Cellar, for all the anti-immigrant sentiment, especially as manifested in the

---

1. Walt Whitman, *Leaves of Grass* (New York: Bantam Books, 2004), 285.
2. John F. Kennedy, *A Nation of Immigrants* (New York: Anti-Defamation League, 1958), 7; it was reissued by Harper & Brothers in 1964, one year after the Kennedy assassination and one year before the passage of the Hart-Cellar Act.

1920s in the passage of restrictive legislation based on national origin, the United States, whether it meant it or not, adopted a self-image of a society composed of a swirling mélange of the world's—mostly Europe's—many peoples. However imperfectly operationalized and manifested in the breach, the idea held sway in popular culture and political behavior, as Americans recalled their own immigration stories and celebrated the nation for its absorptive capacity.

Perhaps nothing represented this better and on a more visible scale than the Statue of Liberty, formally dubbed "Statue of Liberty Enlightening the World," dedicated in 1886 on Bedloe's Island in New York Harbor. The massive "Lady Liberty" had been conceived of and designed as a commemoration of French–American friendship. The campaign to create it, fund it, and place it at that geographic point, where ships coming from Europe made first contact with the United States, had nothing to do with immigration. Yet the poem, to be emblazoned on its base, had everything to do with it and with the Jews. The winner of an 1883 poetry contest happened to be a Jewish woman, Emma Lazarus, who although American born stemmed as did nearly all Americans from immigrant ancestry. Lazarus had written previous works expressing solidarity with the persecuted Jews of Russia, *Songs of a Semite: The Dance to Death and Other Poems* (1882), and "The New Colossus," which posthumously ended up on the base of the Statue of Liberty, stole the statue's theme away from the alliance between the United States and France and transformed it into a paean to immigration.

"Keep, ancient lands, your storied pomp," Lazarus wrote, putting words into the mouth of the statue, whom she dubbed "the Mother of Exiles," as America declared in the now overly familiar and analytically problematic passage:

> Give me your tired, your poor,
> Your huddled masses yearning to breathe free,
> The wretched refuse of your teeming shore.
> Send these, the homeless, tempest-tost to me,
> I lift my lamp beside the golden door!

The officials who supervised the contest and vetted the submissions would have had no particular reason to choose this poem, unless its sentiments conformed to their own. If the theme had not resonated with them as emblematic of America, they surely would not have bestowed their approval on it and helped facilitate the almost immediate process that linked this towering symbol of the nation with the daily flood of immigrants streaming out of steerage.

Over the course of the century and a half after the dedication of the Statue of Liberty and the choice of the Lazarus poem as its core meaning, the United States government and Americans more broadly invoked it as a key symbol of America. Knowing full well that the statue represented the European immigrant experience, official and unofficial depictions of the United States, during World War I and World War II in particular, invoked it as America and by doing so valorized those immigrants in their collectivity as the visible symbol of America. In the early twenty-first century, as anti-immigrant sentiment spiked and the administration of Donald Trump sought to implement policies against immigrants in general and refugees in particular, the image of the statue loomed large as a symbol of the American ideals that seemed to be hanging in the balance.[3]

The fact that the immigrants themselves, as demonstrated so brilliantly decades ago by historian John Higham, captured the imagery of the statue, making it theirs, offers a window into the importance Americans as a whole gave to this phenomenon and the degree to which they recognized, in a positive way, that this force shaped national life, making it different and better than all those "ancient lands" with their "storied pomp."[4]

The importance of immigration for the Jews transcended Lazarus's Jewishness. The fact, staggering in and of itself, that of the Jews who emigrated from Europe in the century between the 1820s and the 1920s, between 80 and 90 percent, nearly one-third of European Jewry, opted for America. America emerged in the European—and to a lesser extent Ottoman—Jewish imagination as a land of wonders, as the best possible destination and the most attractive solution to their problems—poverty mostly but persecution as well. Many of those who went elsewhere, whether Latin America, England, Canada, or South Africa, would have preferred the United States, but circumstances prevented them from doing so. Some destinations for European Jewish immigrants, such as England or Ireland, themselves places of freedom, openness, and liberalism for the Jews, environments offering reasonable economic opportunities, can rightly be seen as corridor communities, places where newly arrived eastern European Jews waited until the chance arose to embark upon their next, better, and permanent move, namely, to America.[5]

"America fever" is a phrase usually associated with the mass exodus of central European Jews in the middle decades of the nineteenth century, as a raging force engulfed the Jews from across the continent, extending from Alsace in the west through the German-speaking lands,

---

3. See chapters 6 and 8 of Edward Berenson, *The Statue of Liberty: A Transatlantic Story* (New Haven: Yale University Press, 2012).

4. John Higham, "The Transformation of the Statue of Liberty," in idem, *Send These to Me: Jews and Other Immigrants in Urban America* (New York: Atheneum, 1975), 78–87.

5. Lloyd Gartner, *The Jewish Immigrant in England, 1870–1914*, 2nd ed. (New York: Simon Publications, 1973). For a recent study of illegal Jewish immigration to America during the decades of immigration restriction, see Libby Garland, *After They Closed the Gates: Jewish Illegal Immigration to the United States, 1921–1965* (Chicago: University of Chicago Press, 2014).

then the Austro-Hungarian and Czarist empires and their successor states. America continued to lure Jews beyond the 1920s, with the end of open and free European immigration. Holocaust survivors waiting to leave the displaced-persons camps hoped to gain admission to America, and hundreds of thousands of Jews, dissatisfied for whatever reason with their actual scripturally promised land, Israel, also turned toward the United States in the decades after the late 1940s.[6]

But more germane here than the sheer numbers and percentages, the fact of immigration as a steady, continuous, and shaping force that made the United States, despite roiling waves of xenophobia and the constantly messy encounters between natives and newcomers, between immigrants from different places competing with one another for jobs, power, and status, and between immigrants and African Americans whose forebears had had no choice in their migrations, left its mark on the Jews who participated in the process. The simple fact, although hardly simple at all, that Jews, like nearly all Americans, had participated in that process gave them a chance on both lived and rhetorical levels to be able to claim that they too, like all, or nearly all, Americans had picked themselves up, abandoned a familiar home, and took the risk to make their way to America. Notably, the only Americans who could not tell their family story as one, however far back in time, in terms of some ancestor who had originated on some distant shore, some foreign land, and with some degree of volition opted for America, happened to be the most stigmatized and persecuted of Americans, namely, the descendants of those who came in chains as slaves from Africa and the native peoples, slaughtered at will by the expanding nation, their land robbed by the settlers, and the survivors hounded from pillar to post until concentrated in the euphemisticly called reservations. In the largest sense, being able to claim, as most Americans could, foreign antecedents offered a degree of prestige.[7]

White European immigrants, exclusively men initially and at long last women as well, experienced the road to citizenship with little difficulty. The Naturalization Act of 1790 set a two-year trial period for the newly arrived European men to proceed from declaration of intent to naturalization to citizenship, but by 1795 the time period went up to five years. Without reciting the details of changing legislation over the course of the centuries, the five years essentially remained in place. The Civil Rights Act of 1866 created the reality of birthright citizenship, as it declared that any-

---

6. Avi Patt, *Finding Home and Homeland: Jewish Youth and Zionism in the Aftermath of the Holocaust* (Detroit, MI: Wayne State University Press, 2009). For more on Holocaust survivors immigrating to the United States, see Beth Cohen, *Case Closed: Holocaust Survivors in Postwar America* (New Brunswick, NJ: Rutgers University Press, 2007); and Leonard Dinnerstein, *America and the Survivors of the Holocaust* (New York: Columbia University Press, 1982).

7. The particular issues involving nonwhite immigrants from Asia will be treated later.

one born in the United States enjoyed immediate citizenship, regardless of where their parents had come from and what they looked like.

Legal citizenship should not be confused with cultural citizenship, a morally ambiguous category that lies beyond the scope of law and state policy. The latter refers to a sense of belonging to the nation, a feeling of being valued and validated by the larger society. But as to the former, Jews like all European immigrants and their descendants, those whose perceived racial identities did not subject them to discriminatory legislation, could define themselves as full participants in American life. Their statements about themselves as full Americans, in both legal and cultural terms, struck a responsive chord with notable Americans, individuals who embodied the nation.

The 1905 commemoration of Jewish settlement in North America took place as pogroms raged in various parts of the Russian Empire, as the British Parliament passed the Aliens Act, and as Jewish immigration to America continued apace; and it provides a reasonable example of how the Jews, as a group, had achieved that cultural citizenship. If any moment in American history should have made Jews, as an overwhelmingly immigrant community, feel vulnerable and foreign, this should have been it.

Yet the programs and ceremonies that Jewish communities around the country staged brought forth broad American support for the Jewish presence. The grand ceremony held at New York's Carnegie Hall on no less meaningful a day than Thanksgiving included such notables as former president Grover Cleveland, secretary of war and future president William Howard Taft, and the mayor of New York City, among others, who showed up to heap praise on the Jews. Cleveland, Taft, and a raft of state and local political figures, along with members of the Protestant clergy, including the bishop of New York's Episcopal Church, journalists, and other notable Americans joined in this and other public festivities, celebrating the Jewish presence in the nation, citing the degree to which their immigrant status did not connote otherness but rather helped the nation fulfill its providential destiny.[8]

Jews, as white immigrants, were not the only ones who merited this kind of celebratory rhetoric. Rather all white European immigrants did, and while the rhetoric of welcome belied the real and quotidian difficulties that immigrants faced and the on-the-ground hostility that shaped many of their encounters with Americans, the nation adopted a set of symbols, phrases, and policies that recognized immigration as having shaped it and made it great.

---

8. *The Two Hundred and Fiftieth Anniversary of the Settlement of the Jews in the United States: Addresses Delivered at Carnegie Hall, New York, on Thanksgiving Day, MCMV, Together with Other Selected Addresses and Proceedings* (New York: New York Co-Operative Society, 1906).

The positive implications of that reality experienced by all white immigrants rippled over onto Jews as immigrants as well. The truth of the nation's long tradition of enunciating welcoming words and enacting similarly beneficent policies for immigrants had nothing to do with Jews, but they benefited from it as did Irish, Scotch, Welsh, Hungarian, Dutch, Norwegian, Greek, Swedish, and and other white immigrants and their children.

While by the early twentieth century Jewish organizations and individuals, including highly placed Jewish communal leaders such as Louis Marshall and Max Kohler, took vigorous stands in favor of immigrant rights and in opposition to the seemingly irreversible path to restriction, the construction of the ideology of the United States as a nation of immigrants constituted an American project and not a Jewish one.

Jews, who in the places they had left functioned as obvious outsiders and as strangers, regardless of how many centuries they had lived there, in America could claim insider status, because in both practical and metaphoric terms, they shared in the national experience of immigration and could point to, with insider pride, the story of their integration. In the telling of their American experience, whether told to themselves or to the larger public, they easily incorporated the fundamental themes of the nation, the themes of Whitman's "Nation of nations" and Kennedy's "nation of immigrants."

The fact that the rhetoric of American life, embodied in the Statue of Liberty and in a slew of texts, programs, and projects, in speeches, sermons, and public pronouncements, celebrated immigration as a fundamental aspect of the nation mattered a great deal. Anti-immigrant sentiment did flourish in America, and examples can be drawn from even before national independence that show that someone or other offered harsh, in fact scurrilous, words about immigrants in general or some particular group specifically. Some Americans organized into voluntary associations that sought to limit the number or type of immigrants, hoping to use their political muscle to accomplish such ends.

Two examples immediately suggest themselves, namely, the American Party, better known by its moniker the Know-Nothing Party, of the 1850s, and the Immigration Restriction League, formed in 1894, an undertaking of descendants of the old New England elite. These two hardly exhaust the list, and historians have amply cataloged the extent and scope of anti-immigrant sentiment that infused American life, resulting in the enactment of restrictive legislation, a slow process that began in the 1880s. And yet, declamations heard at public gatherings and read in an ocean of published works celebrated rather than deprecated the power of immigration, even when speakers and writers pointedly valorized immigrants of the past, say Germans and Scandinavians of the mid-nineteenth century, as opposed to more recent Italian and Slav immigrants of the late nineteenth century.[9]

The fact remained. Americans prided themselves on their immigrant heritage, and America celebrated its history as a place of refuge for Europe's downtrodden. This offers a significant point in terms of thinking about the ways in which America met the Jews. Of the many other migration destinations to which they went over the course of modern history, from the eighteenth century onward, none greeted them with such florid and constant rhetoric about itself as a nation of nations, as a nation of immigrants. Immigrant Jews, leaving central and eastern Europe and the Ottoman Empire, did well in France, the British Isles, Argentina, Cuba, Mexico, South Africa, Australia, among others, but these places, however much they made economic opportunities available which the Jews could seize, no matter the physical safety they enjoyed, and no matter the ability of Jews to function as Jews, creating synagogues, cemeteries, schools, and other communal institutions, they lacked that powerful cultural metaphor that infused America. In America because of that language of "give me your tired, your poor," Jews could handily make a claim, one echoed by others, that they fit into the contours of the national ethos as well as anyone else.

Discourse aside, American realities of immigration rendered the Jews more similar to the population as a whole rather than deviant and notable. At the high-water period of European immigration, the late nineteenth into the early twentieth century, Jews differed little from most of their neighbors as a result of their overwhelmingly foreign birth, their accented and limited (or no) English, and the newness of their American experience. Jews in America mostly settled in a few large cities, living in places where immigrants from a multiplicity of places made their homes as well, rendering urban space in America immigrant space.[10]

Konrad Bercovici's *Around the World in New York* (1924), an excursion through the city by a Rumanian writer, reads like a global, or certainly European, travelogue, as does the more sober *WPA Guide to New York City* (1939). It was not only New York that housed a vast range of immigrants from all over Europe and elsewhere. Chicago, Baltimore, Boston, Pittsburgh, Cleveland, Detroit, Milwaukee, and even smaller cities housed visible enclaves of immigrants from many regions and lands, all of whom spoke their own languages as they acquired English, maintained intra-

---

9. John Higham, *Strangers in the Land: Patterns of American Nativism, 1860–1925* (New Brunswick, NJ: Rutgers University Press, 1982).

10. Alan Kraut, *The Huddled Masses: The Immigrant in American Society, 1880–1921* (Wheeling, IL: Harlan Davidson, 1982); John Bodnar, *The Transplanted: A History of Immigrants in Urban America* (Bloomington: Indiana University Press, 1985.

communal connections through family, work, political, and religious networks, and created cityscapes embellished with signs announcing the fact that Swedes, Greeks, Poles, Hungarians, Germans, Mexicans, Syrians, Italians, and Yiddish-speaking eastern European Jews had all pitched their tents in America. Each city had its own constellation of groups present, in varying proportion to each other and to the American-born English speakers, who themselves had immigrant ancestors. But in their mere presence, they all made the fact of newcomer status hardly notable.[11]

Likewise, the immigrant Jews' American-born children resembled the children of other immigrants, who also stood between parents of non-American nativity and the larger expanses of American culture. Whether comfortable or fraught, their experiences of learning how to navigate the space between the foreignness of their homes and the formal and informal institutions of American life, whether in schools, streets, workplaces, popular culture, and for the men, the military during the two world wars, constituted not a particularly Jewish experience but an American one, endured, and at times enjoyed, by many. Not that all immigrants and their children underwent this adjustment in the same way, at the same rate, and with equal ferocity, but rather they all did so, albeit in their own ways, shaped by a variety of demographic and economic factors.

The great century of migration, from the 1820s through 1924, points to a neat and hardly random coincidence, demonstrating how the history of Jews and of all other European immigrants, coincided. To put it in somewhat metaphoric terms, Jews shared passage with others on first the sailing vessels and then the steamships that plied their way across the Atlantic, all of whom spilled out on to American ports. The stories Jews told about conditions of life on those ships differed little from those told by their co-immigrants, many of whom had actually embarked from the same Baltic seaports. Their descriptions of what it felt like to go through the portals of Ellis Island, opened in 1892, bore a striking resemblance to those of the millions of others who lined up in the great hall, making their way to the desks of the American officials who processed these newcomers. Their story and the Jewish one dovetailed, perfectly.

Jews in America in this context benefited tremendously from the fact that their experience of immigrating from abroad, as speakers of a foreign language or languages, as newcomers to an unknown culture with its own set of rules, put them essentially into sync with the masses of others, and, to a degree, to their benefit removed from them the stigma of otherness.

In this the Jews of America resembled their non-Jewish neighbors in their immigrant status and the immigrant nativity of their parents. In 1900

---

11. Konrad Bercovici, *Around the World in New York* (New York: Appleton-Century, 1924); Federal Writers' Project, *New York City Guide to the Five Boroughs of the Metropolis: Manhattan, Brooklyn, the Bronx, Queens, and Richmond* (New York: Random House, 1939).

and 1910, immigrants made up nearly half the population of New York, Chicago, and the other large cities. If we add to that figure the percentage made up of their American-born children, we understand how urban America constituted an immigrant world and Jews did not in any way differ from those around them. Since no one group dominated the population, of the large cities in particular, Jews like all the other immigrants and their children learned to negotiate America from the reality of this on-the-ground diversity and this on-the-ground novelty. That the official creed, however problematically operationalized, valorized immigration as central to the fulfilling of America's exceptional mission and gave Jews a claim to one key aspect of the nation's central narrative.

This point can be set into some empirical contexts that clarify even further the attractiveness of America for the Jews. Jews, it should be kept in mind, migrated from Europe and the Ottoman Empire to many other countries simultaneously with their migration to America, spreading out from the lands where they had lived for centuries to a series of new worlds. Certain powerful similarities stretched from the United States to other parts of North America, to the British Isles, the Caribbean, Latin America, the Antipodes, and southern Africa, as a transformative modern Jewish migration took shape in the late eighteenth century. It continued essentially unabated, certainly with peaks and valleys, but a centrifugal force continuously pushed Jews out of their places of long-standing residence, operating ferociously until immigration restrictions cut off the possibility of further outward movement, a fact that took a profoundly tragic turn in the 1930s and 1940s.[12]

All of those other destinations lacked America's diversity and intensity of immigration, which in turn made a great deal of difference for the Jews. After all, America constituted the Western world's largest receiver of immigrants from the greatest number of places. Not only did the United States absorb more immigrants than any other place, but the number of those who chose it, according to scholars, probably exceeded the number who went to all the other places combined. Three-fifths of all Europeans who shifted residence across national borders chose the United States.[13]

While Americans, from a number of political perspectives, have generally overstated the degree to which the romance of America propelled the emigration and the uniqueness of America as an immigrant destination and have as such minimized the importance of immigration to the histories of Canada, Brazil, Argentina, Australia, and even Great Britain, the fact remains that immigration to the United States had certain distinctive

12. Hasia Diner, *Roads Taken: The Great Jewish Migrations to the New World and the Peddlers Who Forged the Way* (New Haven: Yale University Press, 2016).

13. Walter Nugent, *Crossings: The Great Transatlantic Migrations, 1870–1914* (Bloomington: Indiana University Press, 1992), 29–30.

characteristics that left their mark on the Jews who participated in this historic transfer of population.

Immigration to the United States differed from all of the flows to all the other places by the sheer diversity of its immigrants. To Brazil and Argentina, for example, two places that immigration shaped and to which, particularly the latter, many Jews went, the vast majority of immigrants came from the Italian peninsula, with Spain and Portugal sending a sizable but decidedly smaller percentage. Of those who chose Canada and Australia, the British Isles sent an overwhelmingly large proportion. Not that these places did not welcome other immigrants, but each one of these places, as well as the British Isles, attracted one or a few groups more intensively than any others.[14]

Yet to the United States, a vast variety of Europeans flowed. None dominated the influx, none shaped the "national character" more than any other, and none embodied, positively or negatively, public consciousness of the idea of the immigrant or the foreigner. While certain decades saw larger and then declining migrations from certain places, over time no one group could be held up as the core population or as the quintessential immigrant outsider. Over the course of the century of migration Italians and Germans arrived in just about equal numbers, and immigrants from eastern Europe more than doubled the number from the British Isles.

Additionally, the flow into the United States proceeded on a continuous basis. For sure, some years, those characterized by a vigorous economy, saw more immigrants make their way to America; and other years, when the economy went into a temporary decline, witnessed a dip in immigration. Certainly the pace of immigration picked up substantially after the 1880s, with the rise of steamship travel, which made immigrant transport a big business. But over the course of the great century of migration, the steady and inexorable process of Europeans choosing America continued apace, with the attractiveness of the migration feeding upon itself. Again this tended to distinguish immigration to the United States from the immigrations to most of these other places, where the process took place over shorter and more limited spans of time.

So, too, the fact that much of the migration to these other places grew out of positivist state policies, undertaken by governments that affirmatively recruited men and women in order to change the demographic or racial profile of the population, providing work opportunities, mostly in agriculture. States like Australia went looking for particular kinds of immigrants, hand-picked them, funded and then settled them, thus deter-

---

14. Roger Daniels, *Coming to America: A History of Immigration and Ethnicity in American Life* (New York: Harper Collins, 1990), 24–25, offers a brief but compelling statistical excursion into the differences between the United States and these other immigrant-receiving societies.

mining the nation's demography from the top down. Many of the new republics of Latin America did so as well, with state officials working to recruit European immigrants, expecting to jumpstart their economies with white newcomers, hoping to offset and outnumber the indigenous population and the descendants of African slaves.

This surely did not happen in the United States, and while some large companies did employ agents to entice potential workers through wall posters, flyers, and other techniques, the American commitment to *laissez-faire*, in which the government maintained a hands-off policy and the recognition that immigrants needed no incentive or prodding to choose America, obviated the need for such practices. Potential immigrants in villages, small towns, and cities across Europe had no need to learn about the United States from agents of the state. They already knew or thought they knew where and what it was.

This had broad implications. No group of Europeans remained unaffected by the lure of America. While some regions sent relatively more immigrants to America than others, American immigration reflected the European continent's diversity.[15]

That diversity had a beneficent impact upon Jewish immigrants, the three million or so who arrived during the great century. On the one hand, no one group dominated public life, and each group had to find ways to collaborate, cooperate, interact, and engage with the other, within the context of the particular people who found themselves in any place. Jews, like all other immigrants, had to find ways to accommodate to Irish, Italians, Poles—their old neighbors from back home, as it were—Germans, and so on, just as those groups had to establish ways of interacting with the Jews. No one of these groups represented the most important immigrant population or the largest. In each case, be it in schools, workplaces, union halls, in the rough and tumble of urban politics, and in quotidian life the tenement buildings of New York's Lower East Side and on the streets of equivalent neighborhoods in others cities, a fluid, ongoing kind of diversification took place, where Jews like other immigrants met, interacted, were in opposition at times, cooperated at other times, with many other peoples.[16]

---

15. Clearly other migrations took place, including across the Pacific from Asia and across the Rio Grande from Mexico. Those migrations will be treated here in the next chapter, which focuses on race and color, inasmuch as these immigrants experienced America in large measure because of the fact that Americans defined them as of something other than white, as members of separate racial groups which called for policies that no Europeans ever endured. See Mae Ngai, *Impossible Subjects: Illegal Immigrants and the Making of Modern America* (Princeton, NJ: Princeton University Press, 2004).

16. This is a history in need of being written. There are hints in the literature about this, but perhaps the best is Daniel Katz, *All Together Different: Yiddish Socialists, Garment Workers, and the Labor Roots of Multiculturalism* (New York: New York University Press, 2011); see

The Irish-American songwriter Edward Harrigan captured that lived immigrant dynamic, played out city by city, experienced street by street, quite nicely in his 1882 song "McNally's Row of Flats," as he described:

> The great conglomeration of men of every nation,
> A Babylonian tower, O it could not equal this.
> Peculiar institution where Brogues without dilution,
> Were rattled off together at McNally's Row of Flats.
> It's Ireland and Italy, Jerusalem and Germany,
> Oh Chinamen and Nagers, and a paradise for cats.

Harrigan, who had no other way of identifying the Jews geographically besides the erroneous vehicle of "Jerusalem," described lower Manhattan as "sort of thick an' mixed like the innards of a mince pie."[17]

During World War II, Hollywood, in direct collaboration with the government and the armed forces, and also indirectly as the studios and their executives shared in the imperative of winning support for the war and participation in the war effort, issued a stream of movies that celebrated the nation's ethnic diversity. These films made the many immigrant antecedents of the boys in the army an American strength. Setting their dramas in the foxholes of the European theater, in battleships on the oceans, and in the jungles of the South Pacific, American movies projected bands of men with distinctive Polish, Italian, Irish, and Jewish names serving with their brothers-in-arms of some kind of British derivation. The scruffy fighters in these films derived their elan and dedication from their united American loyalties and their multi-ethnic origins, celebrating the integrative powers of the United States, which, according to the romance, brought the people of the world—Europe, really—together.[18]

No one of these many groups had the upper hand, and while in some areas of public life, say in the urban politics of many an American city where the Irish had achieved a kind of local gatekeeping superiority over the other latecomers, their dominance did not represent real power, nor did it come to dominate the politics of the nation. And indeed, the particular relationship between the Irish and Jews highlights another characteristic of immigration to America that served the Jews well over time.

---

also Ewa Morawska, "A Replica of the 'Old-Country' Relationship in the Ethnic Niche: East European Jews and Gentiles in Small-Town Western Pennsylvania, 1880s–1930s," *American Jewish History* 77.1 (1987): 27–86.

17. H. A. Williams, *T'was Only an Irishman's Dream: The Image of Ireland and the Irish in American Popular Song Lyrics, 1800–1920* (Urbana: University of Illinois Press, 1996), 168–69.

18. Gary Gerstle, *American Crucible: Race and Nation in the Twentieth Century* (Princeton, NJ: Princeton University Press, 2001), 205; Robert Fleeger, "'Forget All Differences until the Forces of Freedom Are Triumphant': The World War II–Era Quest for Religious and Ethnic Tolerance," *Journal of American Ethnic History* 27.2 (2008): 59–84.

In the discourse launched by nativists from the 1850s onward about the defects of "the immigrants" and in the various crusades to limit the number, types, and rights of immigrants, Jews did not figure centrally. Not that xenophobes ignored the Jews and their seemingly unpleasant characteristics, but Jews never served as the embodiment of "the immigrant" as a frightening figure of the unassimilable alien, bent on taking over and weakening the core of American society.

For one thing, their numbers never reached proportions alarming to the native-born, middle-class white Americans. The three million Jews who came to America over the hundred years of migration stand in contrast to the over four million Italians who arrived in just the few decades between 1890 and World War I. By 1910, about five million immigrants had arrived from Ireland, and in the decades from the 1820s through 1860s they constituted up to one-third of all the foreign-born in the United States. Those years included the period during and immediately after the Great Famine, so the numbers reflect the exigencies of the starvation and deprivation but after 1860 they still made up 15 percent of all newly arriving immigrants. As for Italians, between 1899 and 1924, they arrived two times more often than Jews, although that number obscures the large number of Italians who returned home, as opposed to the Jews, whose migration to America, with few exceptions, represented women and men expecting to settle permanently. Whether the Italians did or did not go back, from the perspective of American immigration officials and the larger American public, Italians—uneducated, prone to violence, associated with organized crime—seemed to be flooding the nation. They would sap the nation's strength and posed a danger for all good law-abiding Americans.[19]

These two groups, each in its own time, stood in the minds of Americans as the living symbols of everything wrong and dangerous about immigration. The Irish and the Italians, at the height of their respective immigrations, exorcized American fears in ways that Jews never did. Each stood in the popular, nativist imagination as the "bad" immigrant, unassimilable, backward, and problematic.

Furthermore, the dense concentration of Jews in New York City meant that even in the other large cities, places like Chicago and Philadelphia, they lived in small enough proportion as to not give fright to Americans fearful of the immigrant invasion, yet in the main in large enough numbers to create the range of community institutions that they wanted. Their numbers for the most part did not loom as a threat to the social order or to the basic composition of the nation.

---

19. Dale Knobel, *Paddy and the Republic: Ethnicity and National in Antebellum America* (Middletown, CT: Wesleyan University Press, 1986); Joseph Cosco, *Imagining Italians: The Clash of Romance and Race in American Perceptions, 1880–1910* (Albany: State University of New York Press, 2004).

But unlike the Irish of the pre–Civil War period and Italians of the late nineteenth century, both of whom functioned as the chief European targets of xenophobic fantasies, Jews attracted relatively little negative attention. Historians of American Jewry have catalogued the words and pictures of the critics of the Jews in great detail, having created the *impression* of a thoroughly anti-Semitic America.[20] But in fact it would be just as easy to cherry pick the primary sources and to locate what in all likelihood would be an equally long and dense compendium of the words and deeds that praised the Jews, the immigrants and those born in the United States, as successful, sober, passionate about education, and hard working, whose presence benefited the nation rather than harmed it.[21]

Without understating the degree to which anti-Jewish rhetoric flourished and how prevalent negative stereotypes of Jews functioned as the stuff of cartoons, stage portrayals, and popular fiction, the bulk of the discourse about Jews as immigrants tended to see them as hard working, studious, adept when it came to entrepreneurship, and set on a course, albeit one perhaps a bit too rapid, toward economic mobility. Americans did not hesitate to dip into the same trove of anti-Jewish rhetoric and graphic imagery that prevailed throughout Christian Europe, but the level of venom hurled at the Irish and Italians, and even more so, immigrants defined as nonwhite such as Mexicans and Chinese, far surpassed that which pointed to the Jews as defective and dangerous to American society.

In the United States, words like "foreigner" or "alien" did not connote Jew. Jews might be included under those usually negative labels, but they did not stand out prominently as representing them. Not so in many of the other destination points for central and eastern European Jews. In those countries, Australia and South Africa, which constituted colonial outposts of larger empires, the Ottoman, Lithuanian, or Polish Jews who came to settle stood out as distinctive for their language, citizenship, and relationship to the imperial project. To South Africa, most other immigrants came from the British Isles, with the exception of those from India, who came through the aegis of the British government, arriving initially as indentured servants. The Jews who went there did not join in a large and diverse flow of Europeans seeking out opportunities in the lands beyond the Cape of Good Hope.[22] For those Jews who opted for Argentina, the overwhelming predominance of Italians as the main immi-

20. Dobkowski, *Tarnished Dream*; Dinnerstein, *Anti-Semitism in America*.

21. The closest detailed study we have of the opposite imagery is Louise Mayo, *The Ambivalent Image: Nineteenth-Century America's Perception of the Jew* (Teaneck, NJ: Fairleigh Dickinson University Press, 1988).

22. Milton Shain, *The Roots of Antisemitism in South Africa* (Charlottesville: University Press of Virginia, 2004).

grant group, quickly constituting the majority of the entire population, and differences in religion and language, made the Jews the obtrusive "others."[23] Even the few thousand Lithuanian Jews who chose to migrate to Ireland in the late nineteenth century found themselves virtually alone as foreigners in a profoundly homogeneous society.[24] And finally, the Jews who moved westward to Germany and Great Britain in the last half of the nineteenth century found themselves relatively alone as occupying the immigrant category. In England, for example, except for colonials from Ireland, Jews made up the largest group of newcomers, the largest category of nonnatives, non-English speakers. In the halls of Parliament and in the press the debate over passage of the Aliens Act at the start of the twentieth century amounted to primarily a debate about the Jews, a referendum on their merits and, mostly, demerits. Jews there and in other non-American-receiving societies, stood out as quintessential immigrants, foreigners, and problems in the construction of a national "type."[25]

Not that those pushing for immigration restriction in the United States embraced the Jews while they rejected other white, European immigrants, but the degree to which the Jews served in their repertoire of concerns as the essence of foreignness paled in comparison to that of the Irish or the Italians. Notably, for example, in the early twentieth century, the Immigration Restriction League and other restrictionists pinned their hopes on a literacy test as a way to keep out the great hordes of immigrants, knowing full well that Jewish men had extremely high rates of literacy, and that even Jewish women, whose ability to read and write fell below that of their brothers and husbands, still ranked higher than that of men from other places.[26] The women and men of the Immigration Restriction League condemned the post-1880s immigrants for their lack of commitment to American freedom, their attraction to America as a place to work and not a place to transform themselves, and as ignorant mostly single men.

Those who advocated curtailing immigration, no doubt, harbored little good will toward Jews or had little good to say about them, but what they had to say about others and what they proposed as a reason to keep them out did not put a particular spotlight on Jews as the problem. In

23. Haim Avni, *Argentina and the Jews: A History of Jewish Immigration* (Tuscaloosa: University of Alabama Press, 1991).

24. Cormac Ó Gráda, *Jewish Ireland in the Age of Joyce: A Socioeconomic History* (Princeton, NJ: Princeton University Press, 2006).

25. Bernard Gainer, *The Aliens Invasion: The Origins of the Aliens Act of 1905* (London: Heinemann Educational Books, 1972); Lloyd Gartner, *The Jewish Immigrant in England, 1870–1914*, 2nd ed. (New York: Simon Publications, 1973).

26. Simon Kuznets, "Immigration of Russian Jews to the United States: Background and Structure," *Perspectives in American History* 9 (1975): 35–126. For a history of the Immigration Restriction League, see Barbara Solomon, *Ancestors and Immigrants: A Changing New England Tradition* (Cambridge, MA: Harvard University Press, 1956).

the main, Americans saw Jews as refugees from persecution, whether true or not, and as such seeking in America the freedom to worship as they chose and to live without fear of physical violence—very different from the imagery of the Italians, Slavs, and other southern and eastern Europeans. American nativists condemned the other newcomers for their lack of economic success and the fact—not true, for sure—that their children, who received so little education, merely replicated their parents' lowly status, again so different from what they imagined about the Jews.

Immigration then as a factor in American life, both on the level of idea and the level of lived reality, enhanced the attractiveness of the United States for the Jews and helps explain the fact that it more than any other possible new home attracted them. Jews living in so many towns and villages in the various empires abroad could see in America a place where they did not function as despised others, as perhaps *the* despised others. They saw a place that for most of its history maintained open, free, and relatively unrestricted entry, for white people, and which made the theme of immigration central to the nation's sense of mission, however problematically worked out. And when they arrived in America, they stood under the protective umbrella with so many others, no less different from them, no more comfortable, welcomed, or valued by the increasingly suspicious core population.

2

Jews Along America's Color Line

Color meant everything in America. The stigma of being defined as nonwhite constituted one of those self-evident truths that began early on and persists into the twenty-first century. From the first footfalls of the Europeans, as they disembarked in Jamestown and Plymouth and every-place in between, up and down the Atlantic seaboard, their whiteness, a fundamental part of their self-definition as civilized, as contrasted with the nonwhiteness of the savage native people, served as the most signifi-cant fault line in the colonies they established. In the key documents that shaped the nation, the Declaration of Independence and, most impor-tantly, the Constitution, color loomed as the binary between free and unfree, between being endowed with rights or existing without rights.[1]

When contemplating the broad contours of American history and try-ing to understand the points of intersection between it and the history of its Jews, the issue of race and color cannot be ignored. Indeed no aspect of American history can be conceptualized without factoring in the deep, wide, and pervasive American obsession with color. The entire history of America has been a history of color and racial classification. This has provided the dominant motif of the national experience, and the very exis-tence of the nation grew out of the encounter of Europeans, native people, and Africans on the shores of North America.

Historians can, and have, rightly postulated that no other factor mat-tered as much, including gender, when it came to the ability of individ-uals not only to participate freely in public life, including access to the ballot box, the assembly hall, or the court room, but also to control their own bodies, travel unimpeded on the nation's roads, and expect that the state and its agents would offer meaningful protection. While gender mat-tered greatly, the fact that white women received a range of opportuni-ties and protections puts their level of victimization at a significantly less harsh or total level.

---

1. Winthrop Jordan, *White over Black: American Attitudes Towards the Negro, 1550–1812* (Williamsburg, VA: Institute of Early American History and Culture, 1968).

To be on the wrong side of the color equation, which obviously meant the nonwhite side, not only subjected individuals to the absence of the privileges that accrued from basic definitions of being human or being a citizen, but it also exposed them to the full fury of the power of the state and society, which served as agents of subjugation and violence. To be considered nonwhite rendered an individual a pesky problem to be solved, a disturbing concern in need of legislation, and a bothersome issue to be considered. Federal judge A. Leon Higginbotham put it succinctly and on target in his book *In the Matter of Color,* which although covering the first two centuries, from the colonial period until the Civil War, his words could, with a few specific changes, extend well beyond the passage of the Thirteenth Amendment, when he wrote, "the entire legal apparatus was used by those with power to establish a solid legal tradition for the absolute enslavement of blacks."[2]

Enduring beyond slavery, this tradition adapted itself handily to include government protection and indeed sponsorship of Jim Crow segregation, police violence, and state policies to suppress black voting even in the twenty-first century. With the end of Reconstruction in the 1870s, the government in Washington bade farewell to any effort to bring about racial equality and enabled the South to handle its special problem however it wanted. By the 1910s the federal government segregated its buildings and offices, mandating after the election of President Woodrow Wilson that African Americans had to eat in separate lunchrooms and relieve themselves in separate bathroom facilities. The American military until 1947 rigidly segregated black men and women, individuals who put their lives on the line during wartime to defend the nation.

In nearly no state, North or South, could African Americans point to a long history of equal rights that provided them with all the formal rights that flowed from the state. As late as 1865, for example, Illinois, a "free state," home of the Great Emancipator, debated the repeal of its black codes, which had for decades barred African Americans from entering the state. The Supreme Court declared in 1856 in the case of *Dred Scott v. Sanders,* with only two dissenting votes, that persons of African heritage could never become citizens of the United States and that the nation's core text, the Constitution, never intended them to be included in the lofty words of "we the people."

The law, the state, and its agents existed to serve white people. Any changes in this fundamental reality required massive effort on the part of the stigmatized and their allies, petitions, lobbying, rowdy demonstrations in the streets, suits in courts of law, and even a civil war that ripped the nation apart.

---

2. A. Leon Higginbotham, *In the Matter of Color: Race and the American Legal Process: The Colonial Period* (New York: Oxford University Press, 1978), 14.

It could be argued, as many scholars have, that the troubling presence of African Americans, first as slaves and then as millions denied civil rights, defined and shaped nearly all important events in the nation's history. The American Revolution, the framing of the Constitution, the War of 1812, the Mexican War of 1848, and obviously the Civil War and everything that followed in its wake cannot be understood apart from the fears, anxieties, and hatreds of white Americans, as they grappled with the matter of race and sought to perpetuate white privilege. A 2016 study of the American Revolution by historian Robert Parkinson persuasively argues that the patriots who launched the movement for independence from Britain effectively stirred up the white public by frightening it with the specter of rebellious slaves and savage Indians should the English not be removed.

Never did Jews, too small in number, too successfully ensconced in the commercial world, and too white and privileged, serve as the rallying cry for political action, nor would any of the nation's momentous events have turned out much differently had they not been present.[3]

Beyond matters of law, policy, and citizenship, African Americans had no choice but to realize that their labor made the nation possible. Being black meant, for the most part, being of slave ancestry; and while by the 1920s a sizable migration of residents of the Caribbean began to take shape, these Jamaicans, Bahamians, Barbadians, and Cubans also owed their presence in the Americas to slavers and their slave ships.

Being black meant that their labor had enabled the European conquest, which in turn led to the American Revolution and the formation of the United States. First tobacco and then "King Cotton," which ruled over an empire of its own, so brilliantly analyzed by historian Sven Beckert, gave the United States its economic dynamism, its reason for being.[4] Even the cod industry of New England took off and flourished because of the need to feed the millions of black slaves being transported to the South and the islands of the British Empire.[5]

To realize the positive draw of America for the Jews of Europe depends also on recognizing that the color divide that invested whites with privilege denied to nonwhites transcended the simple binary of, on the one side, white people of European background and, on the other, black people whose ancestry lay in Africa. Native Americans endured an

---

3. See Alan Taylor, *American Revolutions: A Continental History, 1750–1804* (New York: W. W. Norton, 2016); and Robert G. Parkinson, *The Common Cause: Creating Race and Nation in the American Revolution* (Chapel Hill: University of North Carolina Press, 2016), as just two recent examples of American historians' recognition of how race played a central role in the nation's emergence.

4. Sven Beckert, *Empire of Cotton: A Global History* (New York: Vintage Books, 2014).

5. Mark Kurlansky, *Cod: A Biography of the Fish that Changed the World* (Toronto: Vintage Canada, 1998), 80.

excruciatingly long history characterized by an existence profoundly and negatively shaped by their status as nonwhite people. While their history of massacre and displacement also reflected the fact that their mere physical presence stymied the nation's manifest destiny of continental dominion and economic access to all of its resources, land, lumber, and minerals, their lack of whiteness, as defined by law, made the Americans' land grab so much more justifiable.[6]

American engagement with immigrants from Asia in some ways provides the most powerful way to visualize the Jews' whiteness and the benefits that flowed from it. The Chinese Exclusion Act of 1882 and the designation of the Asiatic Barred Zone in the immigration legislation of 1917 offer the most dramatic examples of how American immigration policy reflected a deep belief in the fundamental difference between the categories of white and nonwhite. These acts of Congress excluded outright potential immigrants from one part of the world, Asia, recognizable to Americans by their phenotype. The Chinese Exclusion Act stayed in place until 1943, when under the exigencies of World War II, as China and the United States found themselves allies in the war against Japan, Congress repealed the offending legislation.

That legislation had much to say about matters beyond immigration, as it specified that no one born in China could ever become a citizen of the United States. One particular U.S. Supreme Court case stands out, a counterpart to *Dred Scott* for Chinese immigrants and their children. In 1927 the court, in *Lum v. Rice,* turned down the request of a group of Chinese parents in the Mississippi Delta to have their children classified as white so that they could attend the better-funded, higher-quality white school rather than be lumped with the neighboring black youngsters, who went to their meagerly funded, poor-quality ones.[7]

The desire of the United States to keep out nonwhite immigrants crept into the conduct of its foreign policy. The 1907 Gentlemen's Agreement, forged by President Theodore Roosevelt and the government of Japan, agreed to stop issuing passports to Japanese who sought entry to the American mainland in exchange for the United States' backing down from a plan to enact exclusionary legislation against them, as it had the Chinese. Roosevelt also agreed to use his influence to prevent the city of San Francisco from segregating children of Japanese background in its public schools.

---

6. Robert Berkhofer, *The White Man's Indian: Images of the American Indian from Columbus to the Present* (New York: Vintage Books, 2011).

7. Erika Lee, *The Making of Asian Americans: A History* (New York: Simon & Schuster, 2015); Charles Payne, "Multicultural Education and Racism in American Schools," *Theory into Practice* 23.2 (1984): 124–31.

In 1934 the United States, in the Tyding-McDuffie Act, provided a road map by which the Philippines might eventually gain its independence, a powerful demand since the 1898 annexation. This promise, though, came with a price tag, one paid by the many poor families of the Philippines, who like their counterparts in Europe had hoped that they could achieve economic stability when some of them would immigrate to the United States and take advantage of opportunities there. However, the plan mandated the immediate cessation of immigration from the islands, a United States territory, in exchange for the sought-after path to independence.[8]

That long, twisted history of Americans' loathing of those defined as nonwhite can hardly be summarized here. Suffice it to say that it infested and infected all of American society and manifested itself in every aspect of public life, formal and informal. Antimiscegenation laws had a robust life in America, not just in the South, forbidding marriages between white people, in need of protection by the state, and black, Asian, and Mexicans, often depicted as sexual predators. The offspring of such unions, these laws implied, fell into a problematic category of mixed race and as such degraded the pretense of racial purity.

The laws of the United States, federal, state, or city, stung no group of Europeans so directly and venomously, and while potential immigrants from countries such as Italy, Greece, or Poland had to contend, after 1924, with the low quotas assigned to their countries, the fact that the law did not name them *per se* demonstrated the difference between whiteness and its absence. Those who came from these places always had the automatic right to naturalize, and their whiteness *ipso facto*, after the requisite number of years of residence, catapulted them into citizenship. No one of those groups could lament to being the chief victim of restrictions on immigration, given that the formula worked out in the National Origins Act took the 1890 census as the ideal moment in ethnic time by which to assign quotas. Jews, like Italians, Hungarians, Greeks, and the others from the newly created countries of eastern and central Europe, could either lament together or celebrate the fact that they had not been named. And, importantly, that legislation did not have an impact on their citizenship or that of their American-born children.

With that citizenship they could and did manipulate the immigration system to bring over family members. They could also use the voting power that their white skin gave them to punish at the ballot box those who deprecated them and reward those who worked on their behalf. They

---

8. On this complex subject of race, color, and the stigmatization of nonwhite immigrants, for example, see Ronald Takaki, *Strangers from a Different Shore* (New York: Penguin, 1989); and Reynolds Scott-Childress, ed., *Race and the Production of American Nationalism* (New York: Garland Publishing, 1999).

could and did run for office and stand up in the halls of Congress and argue for immigrant rights. They sat on juries and decided the innocence or guilt of people of all colors and backgrounds.

This is not the place to dwell at length on the ways in which immigration policy privileged those defined as white, those whose roots lay in Europe. It may be sufficient to say that for most of American history, being defined as white, being considered European mattered greatly in terms of the ability to immigrate, become naturalized, achieve citizenship, and make one's way in the American world. A lively scholarship launched in the 1980s by such American historians as David Roediger, James Barrett, Noel Ignatiev, and Matthew Frye Jacobson have complicated the terms of the discussion, declaring in a number of key works that European immigrants did not arrive actually white but had to earn their coveted pigmentation. These scholars have asserted that it took time for white Americans to consider these people—Irish, Italians, Slavs, Italians, Germans, and yes, Jews—members of the white race. According to this historical trope, the immigrants had to jump through a series of hoops to prove their whiteness, and while the scholars differed among themselves as to how this process took place, when it happened, and if the impetus came from the immigrants themselves or from the larger American public, they agree that whiteness had to be won by those for whom it had been conditional, or not quite white.[9]

While this historical paradigm may have run its course, scholars, including those who write about the history of the Jews in America, continue to invoke a truth that European immigrants, Jews among them, had to, or chose to, become white, accepting as a given the premise that these immigrants fell into some other, nonwhite category. These historians refer, without much thought or nuance, to the proposition that Jews arrived as distinctly less than white and then embarked on a journey, self-imposed or foisted upon them, to secure whiteness, often involving a process of deracination in which they shed their previous loyalties and identities as they cast their affiliation with American white people.[10]

---

9. Matthew Frye Jacobson, *Whiteness of a Different Color: European Immigrants and the Alchemy of Race* (Cambridge, MA: Harvard University Press, 1999); David Roediger, *Wages of Whiteness: Race and the Making of the American Working Class* (New York: Verso, 1999); David Roediger, with James Barrett, "Inbetween Peoples: Race, Nationality, and the 'New' Working Class," *Journal of American Ethnic History* 16.3 (1997): 3–42; Noel Ignatiev, *How the Irish Became White* (New York: Routledge, 1995); Russell Kazal, *Becoming Old Stock: The Paradox of German-American Identity* (Princeton, NJ: Princeton University Press, 1994).

10. Eric Goldstein, *The Price of Whiteness,* is a solid, thoroughly researched and complicated analysis of this, while Karen Brodkin's *How the Jews Became White Folks* stands out for its polemical tone, its highly personal reflections, and unsophisticated analysis. Michael Rogin's *Blackface, White Noise* received a great deal of attention but did little to propel the discourse forward. See Eric Goldstein, *The Price of Whiteness: Jews, Race, and American Identity*

Those who declare that Jews had to become white point to the existence of an American discourse about Jews, as about the Irish, Italians, and so on, that questioned their virtues and highlighted their vices. This discourse, performed in drama, literature, jokes, cartoons, sermons, speeches, and more, extended as far back as the 1650s, when Governor Peter Stuyvesant balked at the idea of allowing the twenty-three women and men who had landed in New Amsterdam to stay, as they belonged to that "accursed race," and continues in early twenty-first-century rants on the Internet that accuse the Jews of so many sins against white America, the real Christians who own the nation. Much of the historical thinking about Jews and whiteness takes as a given that American anti-Semitism, a hard-to-define phenomenon, reflected a belief on the part of some or many non-Jews that the Jews had to become white in order to not be viewed negatively and that hatred of them flowed from the fact that they lacked essential whiteness.

Yet, the anti-Jewish verbiage that Americans created and consumed sprang for the most part from sources that had nothing to do with American ideas about or experiences with color as a pervasive obsession. Nor did it reflect the deeply ingrained belief of most white people in their inherent superiority over black people, or over any other people imagined to be of some "other" color.

This surely can be understood in terms of the reality that anti-Semitism, replete with the words and images of hook-nosed, money-loving Jews, whose hands resembled claws, cropped up in many places where color difference did not exist as a meaningful social divide.[11] Such ideas about Jews thrived in lands where the majority knew of the existence of non-white people only from books and newspapers and not as presences in their own communities.

Little doubt exists that anti-Jewish attitudes and practices found a comfortable home within the Czarist Empire, where a virulent strain of hatred of the Jews swirled among the Lithuanians, Ukrainians, Poles, Moldavians, ethnic Russians, and others who lived there and saw the Jews as a despised group. In this place, from which the majority of those who immigrated to the United States hailed from, the homeland of Jewish forced residence in the Pale of Settlement, of the pogroms, of the educational quotas, and the birthplace of *The Protocols of the Elders of Zion*, Jewish otherness had nothing to do with a white–not white binary.[12]

(Princeton, NJ: Princeton University Press, 2006); Karen Brodkin, *How the Jews Became White Folks and What That Says about Race in America* (New Brunswick, NJ: Rutgers University Press, 2004); Michael Rogin, *Blackface, White Noise: Jewish Immigrants in the Hollywood Melting Pot* (Berkeley: University of California Press, 1998).

11. For more on the development of anti-Jewish iconography and its relation to the exoticization of Jews, see Sara Lipton, *Dark Mirror: The Medieval Origins of Anti-Semitic Iconography* (New York: Metropolitan Books, 2014).

12. See, for example, Hans-Dietrich Löwe, *The Tsars and the Jews: Reform, Reaction,*

An immeasurable portion of anti-Jewish hatred in Europe and America grew out of Christian theology, a deeply believed assumption that the Jews bore the responsibility for the crucifixion, damning them for eternity for their refusal to hear the truth of the good news of the gospel. Doomed to eternal wandering, according to this view, whose origins extended back to late antiquity and eventually gaining traction in modern America, the Jews not only spat on Jesus at Calvary, but their very continued existence as a people mocked his absolute truth and that of Christianity. Additionally, American Catholicism, like its counterparts around the world, declared that the Jews, no different from others who lived outside the only true church, could never expect the blessings of salvation unless they embraced its beliefs and rites.

Other aspects of anti-Jewish practice and talk in America also sprang forth from European roots, the product of centuries of life in which Christian majorities who claimed ancestral rights to some region or another fixated on the Jews' otherness and outsiderness. What with their ghettoes, Jew badges, Jew oaths, expulsions, and massacres, European Christians let Jews know that their differences placed them in a category of their own. Easily carried over to America, but vastly modified, images of Jews as outsiders to the common culture developed independent of the American obsession with color. Americans dipped into a readily available trove of caricatures of Jews: beak-nosed, sunken-chested, beady-eyed, dark complexioned, and sometimes even horned, whose repulsive looks matched perfectly their damaged souls and evil character. These pictures of Jews, with deformed faces and limbs, went back in time to the twelfth century, if not before, revealing the degree to which the Jew's body served deep political and religious purposes and which had nothing to do with America's color consciousness.[13]

The few political disabilities that Jews endured in the prenational period and in the early Republic did not stem from their color but from their religion. That a few colonies and then states among the original thirteen imposed religious qualifications on officeholding put Jews into the same category with others outside of the established church or with nonbelievers. For a few years, Pennsylvania required officeholders to attest to their belief in the divinity of Jesus and to swear an oath on a Christian Bible.[14] A Jew who might do so, or one who chose to convert to Christian-

---

and Antisemitism in Imperial Russia, 1772–1917 (New York: Harwood Academic Publishers, 1993).

13. Sarah Lipton, *Images of Intolerance: The Representation of Jews and Judaism in the Bible Moralisée* (Berkeley: University of California Press, 1999).

14. Eli Faber, *A Time for Planting: The First Migration, 1654–1820*, The Jewish People in America 1 (Baltimore, MD: Johns Hopkins University Press, 1992), 100–101.

ity for whatever reason, would immediately shed his (as women had no traction here at all) disability and be fully entitled.

Anti-Jewish rhetoric in America had a life beyond its religious moorings, and these too existed independent of concerns of white people about the dangers posed by those whom they defined as nonwhite. Here too Americans made use of well-worn ideas developed at times and in places far removed from the United States. The millennia-long association of Jews with money, and the belief that smart Jews who loved wealth and knew much about currencies, gold, silver, and other precious metals could easily, sneakily, buy their way into places they did not belong, inserted itself in the words and actions of America's elite. Jews, many well-placed Americans argued, had risen too rapidly from their poor immigrant antecedents. Now, in the early twentieth century, they stood pounding on the doors of the nation's colleges and universities, its finest hotels and most-refined resorts, its law firms and other prestigious places of professional employment, where work life and social life overlapped and threatened the social order. Affluent white Americans, Protestants in the main, fretted over the possibility that Jews with means could buy homes in their tony neighborhoods and thereby destroy the genteel fabric of community life. They erected barriers such as restrictive covenants, codicils on deeds by which the buyer of a home committed to never selling to Jews.

The well-worn idea that Jews, so adept at money matters, controlled markets and manipulated the lives of the poor also found a home at the lower end of the economic ladder in America as well. Populists, disgruntled farmers of the late nineteenth century, partook in a global discourse about the financial machinations of the Jews, citing people like the Rothschilds, among others, who wreaked havoc on the economic destinies of struggling Christians. African Americans found ways to deploy this rhetoric as well, expressing anger at the Jew peddler, the Jew landlord, the Jew shopkeeper, and the Jew rent collector, linking Jewishness to their asymmetrical economic relationships with individuals who happened to be Jews.

None of this depended on the reality of the American color line to flourish. This antipathy toward Jews and their money did at times spark acts of violence. When times became tough, as during periods of economic dislocation, for example, random, individual Jews found themselves victims of random, individual acts of physical brutality. During the Civil War, the good citizens of Talbotton, Georgia, considered that the handful of Jewish families who lived in their midst must be the cause of their dire straits and threatened to expel them all, including the Straus family, immigrant merchants in town, whose son Oscar would go on to become Secretary of Commerce under Theodore Roosevelt. The threat, however, never went beyond angry words or snarly comments. Jews left or stayed put based on their own sense of place and not on the force of the state, a far cry from the policies meted out by states on those not white.[15]

The most dramatic instance of this, the tragedy of Leo Frank, provides a case in point. The violent death of the Brooklyn-born manager of a pencil factory in Atlanta who found himself at the wrong end of a lynch mob's rope in 1915 did not spark a spate of similar acts, nor did it serve as the opening wedge of a campaign of hatred visited on Jewish homes and shops, in Georgia or elsewhere. Cold comfort, no doubt, to the Frank family and to American Jews horrified at this turn of events, but it did not serve as a harbinger of similar or even worse episodes of anti-Jewish violence. It, like so many other instances of physical assaults on Jews, took place randomly.[16]

Jews in America, the leaders of communal organizations, educators, intellectuals, and the masses of ordinary Jews, certainly worried about the potential for sporadic anti-Jewish acts and anti-Jewish discourse, fearing that they could coalesce into something bigger, more potent, and able to wreak systematic harm. Jews created a variety of programs and projects to defend themselves from defamation and to strengthen Jewish loyalties in the face of a potentially hostile world.

Some of that defense involved a mass project on the part of educators, philanthropists, social workers, and other Jewish activists to wean immigrant Jews of those behaviors that made them obtrusive and different in the eyes of other Americans. Social settlement houses, training schools, agricultural programs, efforts to encourage Jews to move out of New York, classes, programs of all kind, including but hardly limited to language acquisition, as well as exposure to modern and American idioms of art, music, physical education, cooking and child care, involved to some degree the concerns of well-placed American Jews who were eager to lift up immigrants to an American standard. This effort took place not just in the United States, where it might be assumed that it took whitening as its cue, but they also developed in Germany, Poland, England, and the Ottoman Empire, places where the American quagmire of color and race had no salience. In all those other places, well-off Jews took up the task of modernizing and assisting their poorer fellow Jews, and they resembled each other, with obvious national and local variations. These programs,

---

15. Bertram Korn, "Jews and Negro Slavery in the Old South, 1789–1965," reprinted in Jonathan Sarn and Adam Mendelsohn, eds., *Jews and the Civil War: A Reader* (New York: New York University Press, 2010), 116–17.

16. Stephen Hertzberg, *Strangers Within the Gate City: The Jews of Atlanta, 1845–1915* (Philadelphia: Jewish Publication Society, 1978), 200; and chapter 9 of Dinnerstein, *Anti-Semitism in America*.

undertaken in the United States and elsewhere, reflected the Jewish response to the long-drawn-out process launched by Jewish emancipation and integration and not by a desire to make the Jews white.

Many in leadership positions thought that if Jews, particularly the young American-born, felt handicapped by their Jewishness in the American public sphere, they would reject the latter in order to gain access to the former. In the late 1930s, social psychologist Kurt Lewin, a refugee from Nazi Germany, wrote a number of articles for the American Jewish Congress on the topic of "Jewish self-hatred," a trend he perceived among Jewish children in America who had, he claimed, internalized elements of the anti-Semitic rhetoric that had been gaining steam in those years. Nowhere, though, in his writings or in those of the many others who commented on this phenomenon did they cite a wish among Jews to be white. They wanted, according to Lewin and the others, to meld into the American mainstream, and while that no doubt involved a wish to be part of the white mainstream rather than any of the stigmatized nonwhite groups, the overwhelming desire of these "self-haters" involved the wish to achieve middle-class economic comfort without having to endure anti-Jewish limitations and taunts. Lewin, like so many Jewish communal leaders, feared that Jews would find their Jewishness too costly and cease to identify with their community of origin. They could do that, as their color did not hold them back.[17]

The ways in which Jews in America differed from those people defined as nonwhite involved several fundamental characteristics. At no time did the formal apparatus of the society, the state and its agents, declare Jews to be anything but white, and therefore able to acquire naturalization and citizenship because of their color. Their color was white. Never did Jews expect that courts would not protect them when the need arose. They always understood that they would have equal access to the ballot box to voice their opinions and unimpeded freedom of movement. As white men they could engage in all those public acts, sanctioned by the state, that defined citizenship and that unequivocally brought them into the tent of "we, the people," able to own property, enter into contracts, hold office, serve on juries, vote, and all the other basic rights that came with being an American. Never did they have to argue for the right to be white when it came to registering the children for school, applying for jobs, or deciding where to sit on a bus or train. When the time came for some to serve in the military, in the two world wars in particular, they did not get assigned to either "colored" units or Jewish ones. Some of these Jewish young men

---

17. Diner, *Jews of the United States*, 229. For more on Kurt Lewin's writing on Jewish self-hatred, see Kurt Lewin, "Self-Hatred among Jews," *Contemporary Jewish Record* 4 (1941): 219–32.

met rudeness and hostility in their barracks, confronted officers with little love for Jews, but the apparatus of the military never treated them as anything but white.

Their assumed whiteness allowed them, in the eyes of the law, to do what all other white people could do. Rhetoric, particularly common by the last quarter of the nineteenth century, could be heard that questioned the whiteness of the Jews. The rise of scientific racism and the respectable proliferation of biologized views of difference led some writers, thinkers, social scientists, and others to categorize Jews as something other than white, to question the prevailing practice that treated the Jews as white. Tomes authored by American and British writers such as Houston Stewart Chamberlain, Madison Grant, Lothrop Stoddard, E. A. Ross, and a cast of others, many holding respectable university positions, traveled across the Atlantic, launching a conversation about the meaning of the recently coined term "race," and declaring the Jews to be a separate race and as such not eligible for membership in the white race.[18]

However offensive the ideas articulated by these race thinkers, and however hauntingly they came to be implemented in Germany's Nuremberg Laws of 1935, they posed in America a very minor threat to the Jews' privileged access to whiteness. For one, these writers did not limit themselves to considering "race" a matter of white versus two or three other gross categories such as "black" or "Asiatic," but rather they explicated the intricacies of the racial landscape, identifying a multitude of races, including Teutonic, Nordic, Celtic, Latin, Slavic, Saxon, Turko-Tartar, and others, divided and subdivided into a myriad of smaller, subsidiary groupings. They included in their listing the Semitic or Hebrew or Israelite race, terms that Jews themselves used and embraced.[19]

After all, Jews too defined themselves as a separate people, a collectivity bound together by biological ancestry, with membership passed on by birth from mother to child, a standard of biologized Jewish belonging that went back to the time of the Mishnah at the beginning of the Common Era. They too employed the word "race" to describe themselves, considering the word "race" to be related to analogous terms such as "nation" or "people." But unlike the category "nation," that of race carried no poten-

---

18. Examples of these authors' works include Houston Stewart Chamberlin, *The Foundations of the Nineteenth Century*, vols. 1 and 2 (New York: John Lane Company, 1911); Madison Grant, *The Passing of the Great Race, or The Racial Bias of European History*, 4th ed. (New York: Charles Scribner's Sons, 1922); Lothrop Stoddard, *The Rising Tide of Color Against White World-Supremacy* (New York: Charles Scribner's Sons, 1920); and Edward A. Ross, *The Old World in the New* (New York: Century, 1914). For a treatment of these authors in historical context, see Thomas Gossett, *Race: The History of an Idea in America*, new ed. (Oxford: Oxford University Press, 1997).

19. United States Immigration Commission, 1907–1910, *Dictionary of Races and People* (Washington, DC: Government Printing Office, 1911).

tial assertions of split allegiance or loyalty to a place other than America, a visceral concern on the part of some American Jews who nervously witnessed the birth of Zionism at the end of the nineteenth century, a movement that envisioned a Jewish future in which Jews would inhabit, as the title of Theodore Herzl book (1897) states, *The Jewish State.*[20]

Their separateness, Jews argued in the age of Emancipation, did not mean that they could not also become full members of the societies in which they lived, but they rightfully deserved to be recognized as Jews — or Hebrews — a people with a culture, language, history, and family tree of their own. The concept of race worked well in a period of time when Judaism as a religious system came under increasing stress within the Jewish world, what with the rise of Reform and cultural secularism. Since their observance of Jewish law no longer held them together, common ancestry and ancestral distinctiveness could. Late nineteenth- and early twentieth-century American Jews, for example, heartily sung the translated version of the Hebrew Hanukkah hymn "Maoz Tzur" under the English title "Rock of Ages." That popular song included the lines, "Children of the martyr race/Whether free or fettered," which comfortably described themselves and their ancestors as members of a distinctive race.[21]

Discussions about where to place the Jews in the racial mosaic certainly involved discussions of a monolithic Jewish physical "type." The *Dictionary of Races and People,* a forty-one-volume report of the Senate's Immigration Commission, known as the Dillingham Report, stated with utter certitude that such a body part as the "Jewish nose" could be detected.[22] Categorizing Jews as a race also came with a firm belief that each race, Jews included, had its own mental and moral abilities. Senator Henry Cabot Lodge, scion of an old, important, and wealthy Massachusetts family, opposed Louis Brandeis's appointment to the U.S. Supreme Court because of the extent to which the "people's lawyer," who had endeavored to undo the worst effects of capitalism, did so because he had an "oriental mind" and therefore could not fathom the nature of Anglo-Saxon law.[23]

Lodge's assessment of Brandeis's mind, based on his race, fit well with the racialist ideology that pervaded not just the United States but Europe as well. This thinking suffused the broad understanding of how

20. Theodor Herzl, *The Jewish State* (New York: Dover Publications, 1998).

21. For more on Jewish uses of racialized Jewish difference in American history, see Eric Goldstein, "'Different Blood Flows Through Our Veins': Race and Jewish Self-Definition in Late Nineteenth Century America," *American Jewish History* 85.1 (1997): 29–55; and Goldstein, *Price of Whiteness.*

22. United States Immigration Commission, 1907–1910, *Dictionary of Races and People,* 74.

23. Gossett, *Race,* 208.

the world worked. Many races existed, and each one had its own fundamental characteristics. The decision of the U.S. government in 1899 to include the racial classification on required immigration documents and to list Jewish immigrants as "Hebrew" under the "race" column disturbed the leaders of various American Jewish organizations. But notably the category that actually mattered happened to be the one listed under the column of "color," and in that one, Jews got inscribed as "white."

Of even greater significance, the "Hebrew" designation on their immigration documents did not follow the millions of Jewish immigrants into their American lives as they exited steerage and entered the streets of New York, Philadelphia, and the other ports of disembarkation, where they built their communities and would declare their interest in citizenship and political participation.

This does not in any way dismiss the difficulties Jews experienced in America. Exclusionary practices and ugly anti-Jewish rhetoric abounded. Notably though, in the many places where Jews in America suffered limitations and discrimination, in particular in the housing field, in certain areas of employment, in access to higher education, and in entry to places of leisure like hotels, resorts, swim clubs, anti-Jewish behaviors emanated from private individuals and institutions.

These discriminatory places and institutions happened, Jews could note, to be private and not sponsored by the state, not by the official agencies of American government. It would take, in fact, almost the entire course of the 350 years before the federal government wiped away the distinction between discrimination perpetrated by private sources versus discrimination that came from the state. After World War II northern and western states began to enact civil rights laws that mandated that private institutions could not engage in discriminatory behaviors on the basis of religion and race. The 1964 and 1965 Civil Rights Acts made this the law of the land, eliminating the pubic–private divide.

But until then, Jews, as they sought American spaces to live, study, work, and recreate, learned to circumnavigate the universe of private discriminatory institutions and those where being Jewish did not matter or hamper them. They opted for those that welcomed them and in the main avoided those that did not. Where necessary they built their own places of leisure, for example, resorts, hotels, and community centers. As to higher education, probably for them one of the most important sectors of American society that they hoped to enter, unlike their Catholic neighbors, they emphatically never created an alternative system.[24] Rather they took

---

24. Yeshiva College was not created in 1929 as an antidote to discrimination but as a place where traditional Judaism could be taught on an intensive level alongside general university subjects. Brandeis University in 1948 defined itself as a general university under Jewish auspices. For more on Jewish-affiliated institutions of higher education, see Harold

iew gove...

...aratus of the society, its
...eed even its key text, the
...all matters relating to the
...es that flowed from the state,
...e fact that phenotypically other
...y never had to prove it.

...d not legislate against them, limiting
...e in civic life or defining them as others,
...people to be kept apart and at bay. Think-
...e a matter as love and marriage, it becomes
...choice and how Jews had before them ample
...r own desires and social convention. Since the
...America fretted over the personal and com-
...e, witnessed by the scandal that erupted when
...prominent family at New York's Shearith Israel,
...ver Delancey in 1742. But their concerns about
...ross group lines, which only grew as Jews and
...easing opportunities to socialize, mix, and fall
...ne, as they decided on their own, by family,
...ion, how to respond. The state could care less
...t the same time many states affirmatively leg-
...iages or other sexual unions across the color
...U.S. Supreme Court ruled in the aptly named
...ined love and marriage across the boundaries
...e order and demonstrated the importance of
...s always enjoyed.
...epresented in some ways a unique moment in

... percent ...
the percentage of Jew...
ical schools also had a l...
Jewish students they wou...
recounts in his study of Ya...
nitz, the dean of Yale's medica...
admissions committee to "Never ...
Italian Catholics, and take no black...
the chief administrator of the Julius R...
ally, Jews accounted for 18 percent of all ...

No doubt many Jews applied to Harv...
ing institutions and did not get in because ...
qualified Jews who wanted to attend medica...
surely have exceeded either the number the ...
or the figure Embree derived from his researc...
these applicants cannot be dismissed. The re...
candidates had to sting, and their political a...

Wechsler and Paul Ritterband, *Jewish Learning in Amer...
(Bloomington: Indiana University Press, 1994).

25. Harold Weschler, *The Qualified Student: A Hi...
in America, 1870–1970* (New York: John Wiley-Interscie...
woman's Agreement: Jewish Sororities in Postwar Am...
York University, 2013); Jonathan Pollack, "Jewish Prob...
Identities in Conflict at the University of Wisconsin, 1919...
(2001): 161–80.

26. As cited in Gerard N. Burrow, *A History of Ya...
Others* (New Haven: Yale University Press, 2002), 107. Th...

27. Edwin Embree to Julius Rosenwald, February ...
90,12, Fisk University Archives.

advantage of the public universities of the cities and states where they lived, with the City College of New York and Hunter College the most powerful magnets that drew them in. In so many of the cities and states where Jews lived, they found public universities open to them. While on those campuses sororities and fraternities as well as off-campus lodging did exclude Jews, which as private institutions they full well could, the school themselves, operating with the imprimatur of the state, admitted and educated them.[25]

Jewish applicants also learned which private universities did not discriminate, like the University of Chicago, and applied to these in large numbers, winning numerous coveted spots in institutions that had no quotas. When so many private colleges and universities did begin to erect quotas limiting the percentage of Jewish students, starting in full force in the 1920s, those figures far exceeded the percentage of Jews in the nation as a whole. The most famous case involved Harvard, which in 1922 set a limit of 10 percent of its freshman class for Jewish young men, well beyond the percentage of Jews in the United States. Many private law and medical schools also had a hand in categorizing and limiting the number of Jewish students they would take in. In the early 1920s, as Gerard Burrow recounts in his study of Yale University's medical school, Milton Winternitz, the dean of Yale's medical school, and himself Jewish, instructed the admissions committee to "Never admit more than five Jews, take only two Italian Catholics, and take no blacks at all."[26] Yet, in 1931, Edwin Embree, the chief administrator of the Julius Rosenwald Fund, found that, nationally, Jews accounted for 18 percent of all medical students.

No doubt many Jews applied to Harvard and other such discriminating institutions and did not get in because of the quotas. The number of qualified Jews who wanted to attend medical school, Yale included, must surely have exceeded either the number the dean suggested as optimal or the figure Embree derived from his research.[27] The disappointment of these applicants cannot be dismissed. The rejections received by Jewish candidates had to sting, and their political and social choices reflected

---

Wechsler and Paul Ritterband, *Jewish Learning in American Universities: The First Century* (Bloomington: Indiana University Press, 1994).

25. Harold Weschler, *The Qualified Student: A History of Selective College Admission in America, 1870–1970* (New York: John Wiley-Interscience, 1977); Shira Kohn, "A Gentlewoman's Agreement: Jewish Sororities in Postwar America, 1947–1964" (PhD diss., New York University, 2013); Jonathan Pollack, "Jewish Problems: Eastern and Western Jewish Identities in Conflict at the University of Wisconsin, 1919–1941," *American Jewish History* 89.2 (2001): 161–80.

26. As cited in Gerard N. Burrow, *A History of Yale Medical School: Passing Torches to Others* (New Haven: Yale University Press, 2002), 107. Thank you to David Oshinsky.

27. Edwin Embree to Julius Rosenwald, February 14, 1931, Rosenwald Fund Papers, 90,12, Fisk University Archives.

the rejection they experienced. But in larger terms the statistics point to a robust acceptance rate at a time when those defined as nonwhite faced absolute exclusion, as reflected in Yale's medical school admission, finding firmly closed doors solely on the basis of skin color. Julius Rosenwald, retail magnate and philanthropist, who worried about discrimination against Jews in medical school admissions, realized this. He appropriated millions of dollars to build and sustain schools in which aspiring black doctors could receive professional training. He had no need to do so for Jews.

Simply put, being Jewish in America constituted an ambivalent situation, leaning toward the positive rather than the negative. As white people with a full bundle of state-endowed rights, Jews experienced the sting of anti-Jewish practice, perpetrated in pockets, here and there, by individuals and private institutions, acting out whatever social, economic, or religious dislikes moved them.

Jews, unlike African Americans, Americans of Chinese and Japanese ancestry, and Native Americans, never needed to view government, as the embodiment of the nation and the formal apparatus of the society, its courts, its legislature, its elected leaders, and indeed even its key text, the Constitution, as the source of their sorrows. In all matters relating to the fundamental and extensive formal privileges that flowed from the state, the Jews in America benefited from the fact that phenotypically other Americans saw them as white and they never had to prove it.

The nation where they lived did not legislate against them, limiting their opportunities to participate in civic life or defining them as others, as a problem to be solved, as a people to be kept apart and at bay. Thinking, for example, of so intimate a matter as love and marriage, it becomes palpable how color defined choice and how Jews had before them ample choices, limited only by their own desires and social convention. Since the eighteenth century, Jews in America fretted over the personal and communal crisis of intermarriage, witnessed by the scandal that erupted when Phila Franks, daughter of a prominent family at New York's Shearith Israel, ran off with her beloved Oliver Delancey in 1742. But their concerns about the problem of marriage across group lines, which only grew as Jews and non-Jews experienced increasing opportunities to socialize, mix, and fall in love, involved them alone, as they decided on their own, by family, synagogue, and denomination, how to respond. The state could care less about such unions, while at the same time many states affirmatively legislated to criminalize marriages or other sexual unions across the color line. Until 1967 when the U.S. Supreme Court ruled in the aptly named *Loving v. Virginia,* states defined love and marriage across the boundaries of race as affronts to white order and demonstrated the importance of being white, something Jews always enjoyed.

Having this privilege represented in some ways a unique moment in

Jewish history. Here in the United States, for probably the first time, they did not have access to the fewest rights and the sparsest bundle of privileges the society had to offer. Others stood many rungs below them in the scale of entitlement. Here in the United States, they could distinguish between their enemies, particular colleges, particular hotels, particular companies, and the state, the standard of the nation. The former, they condemned for its hostility to the Jews, while the latter, they lauded for the privileges it gave them.

Likely no American Jewish communal figure, no rabbi, no leader of an organization, no activist could have said what Frederick Douglass did on the hundredth anniversary of national independence:

> This Fourth of July is *yours*, not mine. You may rejoice, I must mourn. To drag a man in fetters to the grand illuminated temple of liberty, and call upon him to join in joyous anthems, were inhuman mockery and sacrilegious irony. . . . I am not included within the pale of this glorious anniversary. . . . The blessings in which you, this day rejoice, are not enjoyed in common. . . . The sunlight that brought light and healing to you, has brought stripes and death to me.[28]

In fact, American Jews, the Union of American Hebrew Congregations, the Board of Delegates of American Hebrews, and the B'nai B'rith, the three national Jewish organizations at the time, used that same centennial to solidify their integration, lauding the nation for its inclusion of religious minorities, themselves among those beneficiaries. They waxed eloquently about the capacity of the United States to welcome outsiders and to extend its blessings of liberty to them. Their whiteness, they realized profoundly, mattered. They did not have to say it specifically, but the homage they paid to the United States reflected both the aspiration for continued acceptance and the awareness that no state-sanctioned liabilities limited them. They benefited from their color classification and wanted to make sure it never changed.

Through these organizations the Jews of the United States offered, as their contribution to the great centennial celebration in Philadelphia's Fairmont Park, a statue appropriately entitled Religious Liberty.[29] Keenly aware that they benefited from American realities, including those that accrued to them from the right skin color, some American Jews reacted to the deep and profound stigmatization endured by others, doing so in the context that they themselves faced none of these disabilities. They

---

28. Frederick Douglass, *The Essential Douglass: Selected Writings and Speeches*, ed. Nicholas Buccola (Indianapolis: Hackett Publishing, 2016), 50–71.

29. Diner, *Time for Gathering*, 201–2. For more on public Jewish expressions of civic and national pride, see chapter 2 of Wenger, *History Lessons*.

helped launch the civil rights struggle, for and with black Americans. Jewish organs of public opinion, newspapers and magazines, Yiddish and English, castigated America for its color obsession, taking it to task for its failure to live up to its own creed of equality. Jewish lawyers worked on behalf of Native American, Chinese, and African American plaintiffs who sought to use the courts to press for equality.

That our subjects, American Jews of the past, recognized that they fell on the privileged side of the color line means that the history of the Jews in America cannot be told without linking it to the history of racial privileging. Being seen as white made all the difference for Jews in the positive fit that took place between them and America. America welcomed them as white people.

3

A Faith Community in a Nation of Believers: American Religion Makes a Place for the Jews

Hardly random or capricious, the decision of the B'nai B'rith and the Union of American Hebrew Congregations to sponsor the Religious Liberty statue, as the Jews' contribution to the nation's centennial, represented the organizations' keen insight into the culture and values of their American neighbors. It reflected a strategy as to what they thought would be good for the Jews and how best to claim their presence in the nation's hundredth-anniversary events. The statue, which depicted America embodied in a female figure, defended by an eagle from the snake of "intolerance," linked two powerful American tropes, religion and liberty, and essentially said to the American public, we constitute a religious community, and as such deserve the liberty that we enjoy by virtue of the tradition of religious liberty.

The Jews of the United States made their contribution to the nation's one-hundredth-birthday festivities at a fraught moment in time. In 1863 and then again in 1874, a group of Protestant clergy and laypeople, organized as the National Reform Association, sought to push through an amendment to the U.S. Constitution. The amendment, which never passed although it popped up again in 1896 and 1910, hoped to bring about a major and rare change to the nation's governing document. It wanted the Constitution to declare that as a people, Americans acknowledged:

> Humbly . . . Almighty God as the source of all authority and power in civil government, the Lord Jesus Christ as the Ruler among the nations, His revealed will as the supreme law of the land, in order to constitute a Christian government.[1]

---

1. As cited in Susan Jacoby, *Freethinkers: A History of American Secularism* (New York: Henry Holt and Company, 2004), 105–6.

The amendment movement stumbled and fell and never garnered much public support, but American Jewry considered it possible that it could pass, that America would someday proclaim itself a Christian nation, and that in the process the warm greeting they had received would chill.[2] Adam Kramer, one of the organizers of the "Israelites Centennial Monument" committee, the group that sponsored the Religious Liberty statue, wrote with some trepidation, "We are aware of the attempts being made to insert religious doctrines in the fundamental law of the land." He called upon American Jews to act, to convince the vast Christian majority that "in freedom and harmony there is safety, whilst by a system of intolerance and discord there is danger."

In the face of the threat posed by the amendment, no matter how little support it had, the leadership of American Jewry made a reasonable calculation. In this situation and in so many others throughout the nineteenth and twentieth centuries, it described and presented the Jews as a religious rather than a national entity, as a group of people held together by their ancestral commitment to a set of religious principles, symbols, rituals, and texts. While below the surface of that religiously laced rhetoric they may have acted more like an ethnic group, a word that indeed did not exist until the 1940s, and despite the fact that many Jews had little or no interest in Judaism as a religion, when they showed themselves in public, they did so in the context of a religion. As a community, despite all the internal cleavages and differences among Jews particularly on the matter of religion, on the local and certainly the national levels they for the most part interfaced with the larger American public as a faith community, a collectivity of believers.

Even something as simple as the phenomenon of rabbis being asked to offer benedictions or invocations at high school graduations and other quasi-public gatherings across the country heightened the effect of conceptualizing the Jews as a faith community. Represented by their clergy, the Jews, as residents of cities and towns, participated in civic assemblies alongside their Christian, usually Protestant, counterparts. They took their place, locally and nationally, among the many religious institutions that characterized American life.

Perhaps Thornton Wilder best described the on-the-ground, multi-denominational landscape that came to predominate by the early twentieth century, when his "Stage Manager" character in *Our Town* (1938) sketched out details of life in Grover's Corner, New Hampshire. "Over there," the Stage Manager points out to the audience facing a usually stripped-down stage, "is the Congregational Church, across the street's the Presbyterians. Methodists and Unitarians are over there. Baptists,"

---

2. Naomi Cohen, *Jews in Christian America: The Pursuit of Religious Equality* (Oxford: Oxford University Press, 1992), 69–71.

indicating Wilder's awareness of the class basis of American religious life, "is down in the holla' by the river." And set apart from them all but still part of the landscape of faith in the town, the "Catholic Church is over beyond the tracks," an institution used by the residents of "Polish town" as well as "some Canucks." While Grover's Corner sprang from Wilder's imagination, it reflected a reality of American life. Communities supported a mix of religious groups and denominations. Their churches faced each other, and while they offered their congregants different variants of Christianity, with the exception of the Polish and French-Canadian immigrant Catholics, whom Wilder situated "beyond the tracks" and whose history must be examined on its own, they worked together, lived together, and accepted the premise that religion enhanced civic life.[3]

The religious denominations, both those that immigrants brought with them from abroad as well as the ones created in America over the course of its history, had their origin in a phenomenon that benefited the Jews. While the principle of religious freedom came to be enshrined in the U.S. Constitution, both in the statement that declared that in the new nation there could be no religious test for federal office, enunciated in Article VI, and the much-debated two parts of the First Amendment, which forbade Congress from establishing any religion, on the one hand, and doing anything to prevent the free exercise on the other, the flowering of multiple denominations and religious expressions can also be understood as the result of economic and geographic causes.

The acceptance of the many denominations as a perfectly fine and natural arrangement came into being by default and did not grow out of any ideology from the soil of British North America. Each colony reflected the economic drive of its backers and indirectly of the British government, Crown and Parliament, all eager to wrest a profit from their North American possessions. In order to do so they sought to encourage the arrival of free white laborers who would provide much of the human power needed to fish, farm, hunt, and fell the trees. Other labor systems also suggested themselves, as colonial authorities experimented with efforts to enslave native peoples, invested heavily in African slavery, and brought convict labor from Britain, but these alone did not fill the demand for workers. Enticing white people to voluntarily migrate seemed a perfect solution, and those seventeenth- and eighteenth-century Europeans, whether English, Irish, Scots, Welsh, or German-speakers, all took religion seriously.

These men and women who transplanted to the colonies did so for reasons of pursuing economic opportunity, but like all immigrants they had no wish to surrender their faiths. They expected that if they settled in

---

3. Thornton Wilder, *Our Town: A Play in Three Acts* (New York: Coward-McCann, 1938).

Maryland or Georgia, Pennsylvania or New York, they would be able to pray as they believed they ought to, whether as Presbyterians, Methodists, Baptists, Congregationalists, or Anglicans. Quakers and Anabaptists also joined, finding places to live, material abundance, economic mobility, and the ability to worship as they saw fit. Without that possibility they just would not have gone.

The idea of religious diversity as a positive good took a lengthy time to germinate, as the early republican era witnessed a movement away from religious toleration toward an environment that supported equality of faiths. The historian Chris Beneke has labeled this uneven process one in which "Americans stumbled their way toward something usually called 'pluralism.' "[4]

From the colonial era onward, becoming more pronounced with the passage of time, America needed people to do the work required to develop the land, extract the resources, and make the goods that would sustain the economy. It could not just rely on the voluntary emigration of English Protestants, of either Puritan (Congregational) persuasion to the New England colonies or of Anglican faith to the middle and southern colonies. Indeed, the English colonists themselves represented a variety of religious groupings, different iterations of Protestantism, even in the seventeenth and eighteenth centuries.

While this need for labor inspired America's greatest sin, the forced importation and enslavement of Africans, it also became the catalyst for mass European immigration, which in turn left its mark on the nation's religious life. The need to attract European immigrants to provide the United States with its free, as opposed to enslaved, labor served as the material source of the nation's most prominent and positive characteristics, religious freedom, diversity, and the belief that religion constituted a private matter and as such should not involve the state.

Thomas Jefferson's painful and supportive engagement with slavery has been the subject of much historical scholarship. But he also had much to say and do about the enabling of religious liberty for all. "The legitimate powers of government," he wrote as the author of the First Amendment to the Constitution and of Virginia's Statute for Religious Freedom, "extend to such acts only as are injurious to others." In his *Notes on the State of Virginia,* he continued, "it does me no injury for my neighbor to say there are twenty gods, or no God. It neither picks my pockets nor breaks my legs."[5]

Although Jefferson's vision proved complex to operationalize over the centuries, what with debates and court cases over school prayer, Sunday

---

4. Chris Beneke, *Beyond Toleration: The Religious Origins of American Pluralism* (New York: Oxford University Press, 2006), 7.

5. Thomas Jefferson, *Notes on the State of Virginia, The Portable Jefferson,* ed. Merrill Peterson (New York: Penguin Books, 1975), 210 ("Query XVII: Religion").

closings, the rights of parents to refuse to have their children inoculated against diseases because of their religious beliefs, the use of hallucinogenic drugs in ritual practice, and many more such matters, the basic principle remained. How individuals engaged with the American state lay outside of their spiritual lives, and how they lived their religious lives had no import on their legal status or any connection to the public sphere.[6]

Over the course of American history, women and men from parts of the British Isles other than England, as well as from the German-speaking lands, from Scandinavia, and then from eastern and southern Europe, from China and elsewhere in Asia, from parts of the Western Hemisphere, among others, made their way to America to do the physical work needed to grow the economy, and they brought their own religious traditions with them. Religious homogeneity could never be a desideratum for a nation that sought the labor of free settlers. If America were to have hands and bodies to do the work, then the religions of these many peoples had to be respected or just ignored. A kind of religious pluralism emerged by default. Nonideological, certainly at first, a kaleidoscope of religions had to coexist in order to get the work done.

Notably, one of the first acts of Congress, still under the Articles of Confederation, the Northwest Ordinance, which set the terms by which new lands acquired by the United States would be admitted as territories and then as states, specified the requirement that these conquered lands provide religious freedom. The law, in fact and in so typical an American way, declared that "religion, morality and knowledge, being necessary" for good government and civic harmony should be encouraged. And that encouragement of religion required the untrammeled freedom of women and men to establish the kinds of religious institutions and practices as they saw fit. Likewise, the Naturalization Act of 1790 and all subsequent changes to the matter of who from abroad could immigrate and qualify for citizenship made no mention of religion, indicating by its silence that religion did not matter when it came to such a fundamental state policy.

Jews as adherents to a religious tradition, despite being decidedly *not* Christian, joined in the cast of characters in this American panorama. Even as early as the mid-nineteenth century, rabbis and Protestant ministers exchanged pulpits, particularly on days sacred to the American calendar, such as Thanksgiving and the Fourth of July. Ministers, joined by mayors, other elected officials, and judges attended the dedication of synagogues, sitting solemnly in the pews as rabbis preached, choirs sang in Hebrew, cantors chanted ancient liturgies, and congregants carried aloft Torah scrolls, attesting to the fact that in this town, in this city, Judaism

---

6. Mark Douglas McGarvie, *Law and Religion in American History: Public Values and Private Conscience* (New York: Cambridge University Press, 2016).

had joined with other religious traditions to enrich civic life as it would serve the needs of its members.

Jews as adherents to a religion and as leaders of a religious community participated visibly in public events, whether intended to celebrate the nation or to protest its practices. The *hazzan*, or cantor, of New York's Shearith Israel joined fellow clergymen (he was actually not ordained), marching arm-in-arm with fourteen Protestant ministers in 1789 to mark George Washington's inauguration at Federal Hall.[7] Almost two hundred years later, on August 27, 1963, at a very different kind of public gathering, but one also of great historic import, Rabbi Joachim Prinz of Newark, New Jersey, addressed the throngs gathered along the reflecting pool, arrayed between the Washington Monument and the Lincoln Memorial. Women and men had gathered to protest racism and demand the passage of civil rights legislation, and Rabbi Prinz spoke for the Jews of America. That he had fled Nazi Germany in the 1930s and had served as president of the American Jewish Congress, a decidedly nonreligious Jewish organization, would also have made him an ideal candidate for this role, one that put him on the podium with Reverend Martin Luther King Jr. But the fact that Prinz faced the public as a rabbi and referenced his rabbinical status enabled his community to connect itself to the deeply religious tenor of the freedom movement. Jews, in the 1789 parade and the 1963 protest assembly, faced the American public with their religious personae front and center.

The Jewish encounter with America, one that took place in a relatively harmonious manner, reflected the significance of religion as a factor in American history. Americans for the most part valued and valorized religion. George Washington in his Farewell Address, a document authored by Alexander Hamilton, declared that "religion and morality" provide the "firmest props of the duties of men and citizens," and while he specified no particular denomination or theological stance as better than any other, as a general principle, religion, he believed, "led to political prosperity" and provided the key to the flourishing of "free government."[8]

Americans asserted in word and in deed a belief that religion made people better, provided a good way to organize social life; and because it had behind it no governmental authority, it embodied Americans' equally strong commitment to individualism and voluntarism. Alexis de Tocqueville, the French aristocrat who visited the new nation in the 1830s and recorded his observations in *Democracy in America*, shared with his readers then and with students of American culture for almost two centuries subsequently, how "Upon my arrival in the United States the

---

7. Sarna, *American Judaism*, 40–41.

8. George Washington, *The Farewell Address of George Washington, President of the United States. Dated September 17th, 1796* (Philadelphia: Printed by Henry Sweitzer for Matthew Carey, no. 118, Market-Street, 1800).

religious aspect of the country . . . first struck my eyes. As I prolonged my journey, I noticed the great political consequences that flowed from these new facts."[9]

Tocqueville's observations about religion as a shaping aspect of American life, and as a good one at that, have prompted volumes of analysis and commentary. He contrasted France and America: in the former, "I had always seen the spirit of religion and the spirit of freedom marching in opposite directions." This he contrasted with America, where he "found they were intimately united and that they reigned in common over the country." He believed, as he considered Americans did, that "the safeguard of morality is religion, and morality is the best security of law as well as the surest pledge of freedom."

The Frenchman showed up in America at a particularly notable moment, arriving during America's first age of social reform, when movements galore sprouted to address the plight of the incarcerated, the mentally ill, the blind, the poor, slaves, women, children, drunkards, among others, and all of these movements stemmed from religious zeal. All of these movements invoked the morality of religion to improve society, and all sought to inspire changes in attitude and policy by appeals to moral conscience. The antislavery movement in particular relied on calls to the spirit of morality, based on the belief that a true Christian could not but oppose the enslavement of human beings and that religious fervor should provide the rationale for the call to action. Religion, this movement and all the others particularly of the mid-nineteenth century asserted, had helped make America. It, more than reason, logic, or any other force, provided the basic argument for making it better.[10]

The movements for social and economic betterment that swept America in the mid-nineteenth century and then again during the Progressive Era, spanning approximately the decades from the 1890s through World War I, took place in a transnational context, with similar demands for change sweeping through Europe as well. What made the American iteration of these movements notable, though, involved the degree to which religion and religious rhetoric served as the justification for action. Reformers in America likewise calculated that they had a better chance to sell the public on calls for change through the deployment of religious terminology than by means of any other argument.[11]

---

9. Alexis de Tocqueville, *Democracy in America*, ed. Edward Nolla; trans. James Schleifer (Indianapolis: Liberty Fund, 2010), 479.

10. Alice Felt Tyler, *Freedom's Ferment: Phases of American Social History to 1860* (Minneapolis: University of Minnesota Press, 1944), 473–81.

11. Certainly much of benevolent reform in England also involved deeply religious sentiment, making it in this similar to America, and different from, for example, France where reform movements reflected highly secular impulses.

Religion provided so much of the core of these many reform crusades, with the word not accidental, in part because of its voluntary nature. Women and men in their churches, all of them members by choice who could if they wanted quit and either join some other church or found a new one (or belong to none), had the ability to take religion in whatever direction they found meaningful. Americans, focused on improving society, could take their churches with them as they sought to remake the world. Their clergy for the most part came to understand that they had to move in step with the laity and conjoin their religious activities with efforts to undo social evils.

Religion's deep association in America with morality both reflected and shaped its equally profound association with women. The rise of religious voluntarism, the proliferation of denominations, and the ferment of reform coincided with what historian Ann Douglas dubbed "the feminization of religion," what Linda Kerber labeled the flowering of "republican motherhood," and the birth of Barbara Welter's "cult of true womanhood."[12]

These three intellectual constructs together declared that with the dawn of the nineteenth century, coincident with the Jews' first wave of mass migration, religion slipped into the female zone of concern, and it therefore increasingly involved itself less with doctrine and more with morality, less with salvation and damnation in the hereafter and more with life on earth and the need to extend goodness and mercy to those in need. As churches in East Coast states lost all state support, the status of the ministry declined, and ministers sought allies among women. Historian Mary Ryan showed this transformation in religion and religious sensibilities in her detailed study of Utica, New York, in the mid-nineteenth century, as she documented how ministers of Calvinist backgrounds, who had been steeped in the theology of sin and punishment, predestination and the gaping pits of hell as the inevitable fate of the unsaved, shifted to a religion of love and caring, emphasizing a divine being who bore greater resemblance to a kind father than an exacting judge. In essence, once the divine became associated with gentle kindness, the persona of women arose.[13]

Americans defined women as the more moral of the sexes, the ones more naturally attuned to thinking about the needs of the downtrodden, and the custodians of the morality of their children who would become the next generation of good Americans—if boys, the future citizens and

---

12. Ann Douglas, *The Feminization of American Culture* (New York: Farrar, Straus & Giroux, 1977); Linda Kerber, *Women of the Republic: Intellect and Ideology in Revolutionary America* (Chapel Hill: University of North Carolina Press, 1980); Barbara Welter, "The Cult of True Womanhood: 1820–1860," in *The American Family in Social-Historic Perspective*, ed. Michael Gordon (New York: St. Martin's Press, 1978).

13. Mary Ryan, *Cradle of the Middle Class: The Family in Oneida County, New York, 1790–1865* (Cambridge, UK: Cambridge University Press, 1981), 98–104.

captains of commerce, and if girls, the future mothers of the nation. American women of the early nineteenth century and beyond flocked to churches and synagogues as centers from which to do good work and extend kindness.

Not accidentally, religious groupings, whether local churches or national denominational or interdenominational bodies, provided the core social services available in America to those in need. In a country that took pride in the fact of weak state power and celebrated the reality that government did little for its citizens, churches and religious bodies rushed in to fill the void. Lutherans and Presbyterians, Methodists and Baptists, Catholics, and, yes, Jews, and so many others created hospitals, old-age homes, orphanages, and all the other institutions that dispensed health care, education, and aid for those suffering from whatever kind of distress.

Hospitals in particular offer a striking way that conjoined religion with doing good for all. Americans, particularly in larger cities, could not miss the presence of healing institutions with names like St. Joseph, St. Elizabeth, St. Barnabas, St. Mary, St. Michaels, Presbyterian, Lutheran, Methodist, St. Luke, Deaconess, Mercy—referring to the Sisters of Mercy who built and staffed these facilities—and Mt. Sinai, originally erected as the Jews' Hospital in New York in 1852 and, later in the century, Beth Israel, attesting to the good that religious communities did as they served a public beyond their denominations.

While at certain times and in certain places such good works served overt conversionary ends, in the main they did not. Americans, we might say, associated the names of religious denominations with elementary institutions that served the aged, the orphaned, and the abandoned. By presenting themselves to the public through social service, religious institutions advertised themselves as sources of good, as benevolent and kind, and religion itself as a positive force in the lives of all.

In the time of Tocqueville's *Democracy* and in subsequent generations, religion took its place alongside other voluntary groups, founded by ordinary people as they saw fit. The French observer and so many others after him described Americans as a nation of joiners. "Americans," de Tocqueville claimed, "of all ages, of all conditions, of all minds constantly unite. . . . Americans associate to celebrate holidays, establish seminaries, build inns, erect churches, distribute books, send missionaries to the Antipodes. . . ." Indeed, he topped off this description with a bold comparative statement, claiming, "Wherever at the head of a new undertaking you see the government in France, and in England, a great lord, count on seeing in the United States an association." [14] In this, churches and synagogues as voluntary associations coexisted with the others and essentially competed with them, additionally defanging religion as a force that controlled people's lives.

---

14. De Tocqueville, *Democracy in America*, 896.

Because religion functioned in Tocqueville's time and long afterward as a voluntary aspect of life, as a force of personal and familial choice around which groups organized their social lives, and since it existed independent of state power, clergymen (then women) had no authority beyond moral suasion. As such, anticlericalism never flourished in America as it did in France, and Americans had no need to free themselves from religion if they did not care to join one church or another. America had its share of atheists, and no doubt towns across the country included a handful of those who scoffed at the religions of their neighbors. But they did not function as a political group. Robert Ingersoll, dubbed "the great agnostic," in the nineteenth century delivered lectures on the irrationality of religion, and in the post–World War I period, Clarence Darrow enjoyed great acclaim as a lawyer and spoke publicly about his disdain for religion, while atheist Madalyn Murray O'Hair successfully challenged Bible reading in public schools, winning in the case of *Abington School District v. Schempp* (1963). But as a political force, critics of religion did not organize, nor did they stand a chance against the deeply and pervasively positive power of religion.[15]

The taming of religion, rendering it a voluntary entity supported only by those who wanted it to be a part of their lives, may be the reason that socialism appealed little to Americans. In 1905 the German sociologist and socialist Werner Sombart visited America, hoping to explain why unlike his fellow Germans, American workers tended in the main to turn a cold shoulder to Marxism and calls for collective action in the name of socialist principles. *Why There Is No Socialism in America* offered primarily economic explanations.[16] It offered a gastronomic explanation, commenting on how well American workers ate, feasting often on roast beef and apple pie. We might, however, add that Americans, workers and intellectuals, could not be drawn to the critique of religion inherent in European socialism, arguments articulated from Marx onward that religion existed in large measure as a force that hand in hand with capital kept class disparities in place. A good deal of the appeal of socialism in Europe grew out its association with anticlericalism and involved a critique of a reality that religious authorities who derived their power from the state combined to keep the poor in poverty and the rich in power.

The American poor actually created their own churches, founding thousands of religious institutions, storefront churches, tent cities, miniscule chapels, and sanctuary buildings that they organized, paid for,

---

15. A recent history of atheism in America is Leigh Eric Schmidt, *Village Atheists: How America's Unbelievers Made Their Way in a Godly Nation* (Princeton, NJ: Princeton University Press, 2016).

16. Werner Sombart, *Why Is There No Socialism in the United States?* (White Plains, NY: International Arts and Sciences Press, 1976).

and worshiped in as they saw fit. Religion functioned as one of the few aspects of their lives that they could shape and control, independent of the employers who used their labor and exploited them. Ministers who officiated in grand religious edifices, educated at elite institutions of higher learning, and ordained by well-heeled denominations had no more or less power or authority in the eyes of the state than did Phoebe Smith, Elijah Muhammad, Billy Sunday, Aimee Semple McPherson, Father Divine, and the other religious leaders who rose to prominence because some number of "plain folk" flocked to them, invested authority in them, and aided them in their work.[17]

Not surprising in this context, then, America functioned as a hothouse for the growing of new religions, some of which became major religious bodies: the African Methodist Episcopal Church, the Seventh Day Adventists, the Church of Jesus Christ of Latter Day Saints (Mormonism) as well as Christian Science, the Disciples of Christ, and the Hare Krishnas, just a few examples of those religious groups that persisted and flourished, among the many others that enjoyed brief moments in the sun.[18] New religions, like old ones, competed with one another in the American marketplace of the spirit. If the founders and leaders of these new churches articulated compelling messages and provided meaningful social spaces, they endured. If they did not, they died. But while they lived, they had the same rights as the clergy of old, well-known denominations whose histories extended back in time.

Churches once unified and solidly constructed around a leadership and theological core fractured in America as men and women, clergy and laity, sought to worship in places that represented their social and cultural values. By the latter part of the nineteenth century, fifty-eight different Lutheran synods existed in the United States, each one representing not just the essence of the teachings of Martin Luther but the place of origin from which congregants hailed, the language they believed essential to engaging with the divine, as well as how they interpreted the true meaning of the faith tradition. By 1917, when some within the Lutheran world in the United States began to articulate the need to overcome such splintering, no fewer than 150 different iterations of Lutheranism had come into being, flowered, and competed with one another. Each brand of Lutheranism, however, exercised the same authority over its members, doing

---

17. Liston Pope, *Millhands & Preachers: A Study of Gastonia* (New Haven: Yale University Press, 1944). Useful studies of fundamentalism in America include George Marsden, *Fundamentalism and American Culture*, 2nd ed. (Oxford: Oxford University Press, 2006); and Joel Carpenter, *Revive Us Again: The Reawakening of American Fundamentalism* (Oxford: Oxford University Press, 1997).

18. Darren Dochuk, *From Bible Belt to Sunbelt: Plain-Folk Religion, Grassroots Politics, and the Rise of Evangelical Conservatism* (New York: W. W. Norton & Company, 2011).

so only on a voluntary basis; and each drew the same recognition from the state, basically none, with the exception of enjoying tax-free status for their buildings, seminaries, and other facilities.

From the perspective of the laity, religion existed as something that women and men, those who filled the pews, paid the dues of, held title to the buildings of, positively chose to be part of, as they liked. As for the clergy, they had no choice but to hone their speaking and pastoral skills so that they could attract members who would then pay their salaries, listen to their sermons, and follow their teachings. That religion became liberated of the state and the state left religions on their own solidified the popular understanding in America that linked religion with civic good and moral benevolence, just as Washington had articulated as he bade farewell to the nation when he left office.

The idea of religion as something of value infused American life. While this became particularly salient during the Cold War, when the United States positioned itself against the godless communism of the Soviet Union and its satellite states, announcing instead that it consti- tuted "one nation under God" in the Pledge of Allegiance, which most school children had to recite—little hands over their hearts—such think- ing long predated that era. The Civil War, undertaken by the United States to preserve the union and end slavery, cannot be understood without its flamboyant religious imagery. Julia Ward Howe's "Battle Hymn of the Republic" resounded with the repeated chorus, "His truth is marching on." Its final verse declared that just as he, Jesus, "died to make men holy, let us die to make men free."[19]

The history of Jewish chaplaincy in the military provides a fine exam- ple of the evolution of Jewish religious privilege, demonstrating the arc of integration that went hand in hand with the increase in the number of Jews in America. With the outbreak of the Civil War, Congress gave over- sight of the chaplaincy to the Y.M.C.A., the Young Men's Christian Asso- ciation, an evangelically oriented body established a decade earlier, which sent field agents to visit the troops and see to their needs. The legislation had specifically mandated that a chaplain had to be an ordained minister in a Christian denomination, but the men in their regiments voted for their own chaplains. The 65th Regiment of Pennsylvania's Fifth Cavalry voted in as its spiritual guide Sergeant Michael Allen, a Hebrew teacher who had studied for the rabbinate but had never been ordained. Upon learning of Allen's appointment, the Y.M.C.A. field worker threatened him with dis- honorable discharge, and he resigned. The regiment, however, followed

---

19. On the change in the Pledge of Allegiance, see Kevin Krause, *One Nation under God: How Corporate America Invented Christian America* (New York: Basic Books, 2015), 95–126. For more on lyric changes in the "Battle Hymn of the Republic," see Edmund Wilson, *Patriotic Gore: Studies in the Literature of the American Civil War* (New York: W. W. Norton, 1994), 59–98.

up and elected in his stead Arnold Fischel, an ordained rabbi associated with New York's Shearith Israel congregation. Fischel applied to the War Department for his commission, which turned him down. A flurry of letters, protests, sermons, and petitions changed the policy.[20]

But with the United States' entry into World War I in 1917, the War Department created a very different kind of reality. It still felt the need to oversee the religious lives of the masses of men who had been drafted and still believed that caring for their religious lives would enhance their moral fiber and their morale. But by 1917 the military decided to give the Y.M.C.A. oversight only of the Protestant men. The Knights of Columbus would take care of the Catholics in uniform, and the newly created Jewish Welfare Board would minister to the young Jewish men who helped to make the world safe for democracy. The three organizations, representing the three religious groupings, despite their disparate sizes, functioned together, base by base, military camp by military camp.[21] While this did not take place without conflict and competition, in the main the Jewish, Protestant, and Catholic clergy found ways to work together for what they defined as the common good of the men, to help the Allies win the war, and to do the bidding of the War Department.

Even more during World War II, a conflict that lasted so much longer and involved so much larger a military force, the chaplains, regardless of denomination, ministered to the men across religious lines, shared resources, and forged what would emerge in common parlance in the aftermath of the war as "tri-faith America," a nation made up of, as the title of Will Herberg's book (1955) stated, Catholic-Protestant-Jew.[22]

That Judaism, the smallest of the three by far, got included in this triple crown of American religion in and of itself provides a noteworthy way of thinking about the synergistic relationship between Jews and America through the agency of religion. Analysts of American religion, as well as presidents and other public figures, who spoke in reverential terms about America's religious landscape, could very easily have described it as a Christian nation, or perhaps as a society made up of Protestants and Catholics. But the fact that by the early twentieth century they opted for rhetoric that focused on the three religions of the American people says much about the ways in which Americans, even as they discriminated against

---

20. A brief retelling of the "chaplain controversy" can be found in Diner, *Time for Gathering*, 157–58. For additional source material, see Bertram Korn, "Jewish Chaplains during the Civil War," *American Jewish Archives Journal* 1.1 (1948): 6–7; and Louis Barish, "The American Jewish Chaplaincy," *American Jewish Historical Quarterly* 52.1 (1962): 9–11.

21. Jessica Cooperman, "The Jewish Welfare Board and Religious Pluralism in the American Military of World War I," *American Jewish History* 98.4 (2014): 237–61.

22. Will Herberg, *Protestant–Catholic–Jew: An Essay in American Religious Sociology* (Garden City, NY: Doubleday, 1955); Kevin Schultz, *Tri-Faith America: How Catholics and Jews Held Postwar America to Its Protestant Promise* (Oxford: Oxford University Press, 2011).

Jews in housing, private higher education, places of recreation, and certain forms of elite employment, still celebrated the inclusion of Judaism in the religious pantheon of the nation.

While Jews and Jewish texts may not actually separate out something called "religion" from the idea of Israel as a people, bound to one other across time and space, Americans for the most part, because of the Protestant origins of the nation, considered religion and peoplehood two very different entities, and Americans, as Tocqueville and so many others declared, conceived of religion in general as a good thing. They had much more difficulty with the idea of loyalty to some other land, to some foreign entity. Not until the latter part of the twentieth century did the United States allow for dual citizenship; upon taking their oaths to become citizens, immigrants had to forswear allegiance to any other government, and Americans had no difficulty labeling things, people, and ideas that they did not like as "un-American."

And for the most part, when Jews pressed for greater inclusion, for the nation to live up to its ideals, they did so in the name of their religion, rather than for something we might conceive of as group or ethnic rights. Their campaign against the Christian Nation Amendment provides a revealing case in point. So too their protests during the Civil War of the exclusion of Jewish clergy from the chaplaincy demonstrate the degree to which they embarked on the path for equality through the medium of religion. Give Judaism, they argued, the same rights and privileges that Christianity enjoyed. Nothing to Jews, they basically declared, as a people, an ethnic group, or a national entity, but to Jews as the bearers of a religion no less worthy than Christians, everything.

The religious sphere also provided American Jews, rabbis in particular, with a prominent place in which to showcase their religion and help make life more comfortable. The field of interfaith or interreligious work took off in the 1920s, and in organizations like the National Conference of Christians and Jews, founded in part to counteract growing anti-Semitism and xenophobia, embodied in the growing popularity of the newly resurrected Ku Klux Klan, Catholic, Protestant, and Jewish clergy established personal connections with one another as they sought to teach the American public about the importance of tolerance. The National Conference sent out across the country carefully selected trios, each one made up of a rabbi, a priest, and a minister, to speak to community groups and to emphasize the fundamental commonalities of all religions, or at least Western ones, despite doctrinal differences.[23]

Such undertakings continued into the 1930s and 1940s, as fascism and Nazism threatened the Jews and Americans' liberal vision of human prog-

---

23. Schultz, *Tri-Faith America*, 31–32.

ress. Jews, seeing the importance of such work, garnered a great deal of cooperation in goodwill, and two projects in particular at the Conservative movement's Jewish Theological Seminary solidified bonds between Jewish and Christian clergy. The Institute for Religion and Social Studies, founded in 1938, and the Conference on Science, Philosophy and Religion and Their Relationship to the Democratic Way of Life (1940), both founded by seminary chancellor Rabbi Louis Finkelstein, incorporated the clergy and intellectual luminaries of the faith communities into ongoing dialogue with one another.

In these and other interfaith enterprises representatives of the Jewish, Catholic, and Protestant religious communities in America, on both the national and the local level, found ways to work with one another, seeking to undermine hatreds inherited from the past, as they addressed immediate problems. They all claimed to be serving America, and ultimately the world at large, by operating together, where and when they could.

The American Catholic prelates who took part in the mid-1960s at the Second Vatican Council, or Vatican II, spearheaded a fundamental shift in Catholic–Jewish relationships, at least on a theological level, and their activism reflected the interfaith work that they had been involved with in their home communities. They, after decades of interfaith cooperation with their Jewish counterparts, played a pivotal role in getting the council to rethink the church's centuries' old castigation of the Jews as those responsible for the crucifixion. They succeeded, in concert with a number of Jewish religious leaders, such as Rabbi Abraham Joshua Heschel, to formulate *Nostra aetate*, issued in October 1965, which proclaimed, "His passion cannot be charged against all Jews . . . then alive, nor against the Jews of today." Furthermore the document gave official approval to the kinds of interfaith conversations that had been taking place in America for, at that point, four decades, as it stated, the "spiritual patrimony common to Christians and Jews is thus so great" that "this sacred synod wants to foster and recommend that mutual understanding and respect which is the fruit . . . of biblical and theological studies as well as of fraternal dialogues." Not coincidentally, Americans played the pivotal role in this transformation, and Jews considered that they benefited from this easing of the church's historic position.[24]

Jewish religious life in America did not start quite so auspiciously, but even in its initial inauspiciousness some of these basic themes emerged. The often-told story of Peter Stuyvesant shows us this. He had no interest in allowing the Jews to remain in New Amsterdam but had to respect

---

24. James Rudin, *Cushing, Spellman, O'Connor: The Surprising Story of How Three American Cardinals Transformed Catholic–Jewish Relations* (Grand Rapids, MI: W. B. Eerdmans, 2012), 110–13.

the directives of the Dutch West India Company, which owned the colony and had ruled that the Jews could stay. However, among a few other restrictions that they placed on them, company officials decreed that the Jews could not pray in public. They had to, essentially, reserve their religious activities for private spaces, which in fact posed no problem for Jews, inasmuch as they did not require a formally designated building called a synagogue in which to conduct their religious activities.

The New Amsterdam story serves not as an exception to the larger point here about religion working for the Jews in America rather than against them. For one, Lutherans had been forbidden from even praying in private while Jews could do religiously whatever they wanted if they kept themselves out of the public eye. Catholics could not step foot on the soil of the Dutch Reformed colony. More significantly, when under the leadership of Asser Levy the Jews appealed to Stuyvesant, they did so not to repeal the ban on public worship but to purchase and consecrate a plot of land for a cemetery. He agreed to that, and whether he knew it or not, the presence of a consecrated burial ground mattered more to Jews as a religious site than any building might.

Finally, the days of Dutch rule of the island were numbered, and within ten years of the arrival of the Jews, the British came, saw, and conquered, changing the name of the settlement to New York. From then on, and in all of the colonies where Jews settled, they organized congregations when and how they wanted. In the Atlantic seaboard cities of Newport, New York, Philadelphia, Savannah, and Charleston, Jews as a religious community organized their religious lives in ways that they chose, hampered only by their small numbers and the vast distances that separated them from large centers of Jewish life where sacred books, ritual objects, and authoritative religious personnel could be found.

The thrust of religious life in America, colonial and beyond, worked well for the Jews as they arrived and planted themselves in the nation. Few examples exist of Christians organizing to oppose the opening and chartering of synagogues in their communities, or of Jews experiencing religious discrimination. Only in New England in the colonial era can one talk about the creation of barriers to the practice of Judaism, and since few Jews settled there before the 1840s and 1850s, it touched few as a negative force. During the colonial period, the Puritan settlers of Connecticut in the 1650s, for example, had secured a royal charter for the colony, which barred Jews from building a synagogue or buying land for a cemetery, although it ought to be noted that Anglicans, communicants in the Church of England, could not, by law, worship publicly until the 1720s, despite England's role as the colonial governing power. Quakers and Baptists lived in the colony with only limited tolerance, and Catholics could not be present there at all.

Even into the era of the American Revolution, Americans initially stood by their denomination, expressing disdain for the ones they did not belong to, evincing hostility toward the others. But by the time of the early republic and then developing with the growth of the population and the movement westward, denominational rivalries faded in significance. Theologians and officials of particular churches may have continued to argue for the rightness of their particular interpretations, rituals, and structures, but on the ground American Protestants glided from church to church, moving their membership from denomination to denomination, just as they moved from state to state, from town to town. Mobility from faith community to faith community blurred meaningful doctrinal differences.

This mobility of faith and acceptance of diversity grew with time and helps explain the evolving normalization, indeed validation, of Judaism. The history of limitations on the practice of Judaism during the colonial era in New England, again like the Stuyvesant story, to a large degree proves the point of America's warm reception of the Jews through the religious context. Limited to just a few colonies, Jews in Connecticut, Massachusetts, and New Hampshire suffered limitations on their right to act religiously as Jews but did so no differently from others who did not belong to the established church. Lumped together with all others who did not join in the fellowship of the Congregational churches, sit in the pews on Sunday mornings, and listen to the words of these ministers, increasingly the graduates of Harvard and Yale colleges, the Jews endured the limitations imposed on all religious outsiders. For the relatively few Jews who actually lived in these colonies, and then states of the early republic, it lasted a relatively short span of years. Although the full disestablishment of religion in Connecticut and Massachusetts did not come to fruition until the 1820s, bans on Jewish worship and restrictions on their settlement and ability to fulfill their religious obligations petered out well before then. And, in every other colony where Jews sought to live, doing so for strategic economic reasons, they built synagogues, dedicated cemeteries to bury their dead, taught religious precepts to their children, circumcised their sons, married, baked *matzah* for Passover, procured kosher meat, and lived as Jews, which largely meant religiously.

Despite the strongly Christian tenor of life, the Jews' arrival and settlement in America stimulated little public concern or discussion. The uncomplicated process by which they purchased land for cemeteries and synagogue buildings, for example, caused no governmental body or agitated group of citizens to comment on the potential problems that might ensue, as this decidedly non-Christian group set down roots and joined the local roster of churches, Presbyterian, Methodist, Episcopalian, Lutheran, Congregational, Baptist, Disciples of Christ, and so on. Thornton Wilder did not mention a Jewish presence in his fictional Grover's Corner, but around the country synagogues bloomed and local boosters pointed with pride, on their town maps and other documents, to the presence of the synagogue as a prominent institution. In 1864, for example, the city of Madison, Wisconsin, prominently featured Congregation Shaarei Shamayim in an official lithograph depicting the city's important buildings. While only twenty Jewish families made their home in the state capitol, "A View from Madison" made the Jewish religious presence a notable fact in presenting itself as a place of robust growth and prosperity.[25]

At other times and in other places, local town and city boosters considered the forming of a Jewish congregation a sign of both cosmopolitanism and the beginnings of a business boom. In the 1870s, after a number of failed attempts to create a permanent Jewish religious institution in Austin, Texas, a local newspaper commented, "we can see no reason why Austin should not keep company" with the other cities in the state, like Galveston, Dallas, and Houston, that could already claim that synagogues or at least Jewish congregations existed and flourished within their town lines.

Such a call by a local newspaper, intended to stimulate the Jews to organize themselves into a permanent religious institution, may have been unusual, but the formation of congregations and the opening of Jewish houses of worship caused no negative reactions. At best ignored, the Jews as individuals mostly took up positions as shopkeepers, and more often than not, the men joined local Masonic lodges, held minor political offices, while their children attended public schools. The Jewish congregation in Port Gibson, Mississippi, or Port Jervis, New Jersey, in Portland, Maine, and Portland, Oregon, appeared on town maps and in local directories, and as best we can know, their neighbors merely considered these the places where their Jewish neighbors worshiped and held their life-cycle events.

Judaism became part of the religious or denominational landscape of the Jews' chosen cities and towns. What privileges churches and Christian congregations enjoyed, synagogues did as well, with the exemption from property taxes a not insignificant benefit for all. What respect Christian ministers enjoyed, rabbis did as well. When in 1924 Congress passed quite draconian immigration legislation severely curtailing the number of immigrants who could come to America, and doing so on the basis of

---

25. Wisconsin Historical Society, Louis Kurz, *Gates of Heaven Synagogue*, ID #36491. Online at http://www.wisconsinhistory.org/Content.aspx?dsNav=Ny:True,Ro:0,N:4294963 828–4294955414&dsNavOnly=Ntk:All%7cshaaray%7c3%7c,Ny:True,Ro:0&dsRecord Details=R:IM36491&dsDimensionSearch=D:synagogue,Dxm:All,Dxp:3&dsCompound DimensionSearch=D:synagogue,Dxm:All,Dxp:3, accessed October 24, 2016. The image also appears in Diner, *Time for Gathering*, illustration facing p. 141.

national origin, it exempted clergymen from the restrictions. Rabbis, like Catholic priests and nuns, Greek Orthodox prelates, or Protestant ministers, could come to the United States even if their compatriots faced severe limitations, attesting to the prevailing view of religion as something worth fostering. The role of rabbis in public ceremonies, like those with which this chapter began and so many more, giving the benediction at the opening of a congress or a state legislature, for example, attested to the honor bestowed on Jewish clergy, putting them on a par with their Christian counterparts.

At a very different level but also reflecting that same positive value assigned to religion, by the 1920s the Boy Scouts of America, eager to enroll Jewish youngsters, at the behest of Jewish community leaders gave official sanction to the bestowing of the Ner Tamid Award, a badge to be sewn on a Jewish boy's uniform in recognition of his performance of Jewish religious acts. Named for the eternal flame that flickers in synagogues in front of the ark containing the Torah scrolls, the Boy Scouts of America helped transform Jewish obligations, *mitzvoth,* into American badges of honor.[26]

This valorization of Jews through Judaism might be read in one very small comment, but one that reveals much about Jewish life at a local level. Julius Rosenwald, who grew up in the small Jewish community of Springfield, Illinois, in the 1860s and 1870s, remarked once, well after he had become a great retail magnate and an extraordinary philanthropist to Jewish and African-American undertakings, "I always believed that the respect in which the Jews of Springfield were held by their Christian fellows was largely the result of the congregational life," and he went on to state that "the Rabbi represented the Jews when an occasion arose."[27]

Not only did Rosenwald remember his Springfield boyhood this way, but the career biographies of American rabbis and the histories of Jewish congregations from the middle of the nineteenth century onward include a trove of details about the rabbis' participation in civic events and their presence at interdenominational gatherings. In 1876, for example, an early rabbi of Detroit's Beth El congregation, Rabbi Leopold Wintner accepted an invitation to preach at the Church of Our Father, and, according to a short history of Beth El, "since that year there has been a continuous interchange of pulpits between our rabbis and the Christian ministers in the community." A later rabbi of Beth El, probably its most famous, Leo M.

---

26. "A Scout Is Reverent," *Boys' Life: For All Boys* (February 1963): 35. For more on how Jews and other minorities fared in the Boy Scouts, see Benjamin Jordan, *Modern Manhood and the Boy Scouts of America: Citizenship, Race and the Environment, 1910–1930* (Chapel Hill: University of North Carolina Press, 2016).

27. Hasia Diner, *Julius Rosenwald: A Very Lucky Jewish Life* (New Haven: Yale University Press, forthcoming).

Franklin, developed an intense set of civic involvements that stretched beyond the Jewish community, and, "there has been no social, civic, or philanthropic movement," according to the congregational history, in which he did not participate. For that, "he was honored for his work by the award of an Honorary Doctor of Laws degree by the University of Detroit, a Catholic institution; an Honorary Doctor of Laws degree by Wayne ... University; a citation for distinguished living by the Detroit Round Table of Catholics, Jews, and Protestants; and by election at three different periods as President of the Detroit Public Library Commission." [28]

As a result of that respect, enhanced by that rabbinic representation and reflecting the basic workings of the constitutional system, with all the benefits that accrued to congregations, that is, Christian ones, synagogues fared no differently. Congress, for example, as it administered the affairs of the District of Columbia had passed an act in 1844 by which title for real estate could be conveyed to the trustees of churches. It did not mention synagogues because no Jews lived or worshiped there. When the Washington Hebrew Congregation sought to incorporate in the 1850s, its founders turned to Jonas P. Levy, a Mexican War hero, to use his political contacts to help them circumvent the language that would seem to exclude them. In 1856, with little controversy or discussion, Congress passed "An Act for the Benefit of the Hebrew Congregation of the City of Washington," giving the fledgling congregation and all others that would follow all the rights and privileges enjoyed by Christian churches.[29]

The history of synagogue buildings in America, in communities large and small, testifies to this as well. While until the 1840s synagogue buildings eschewed signs, symbols, and words on their exteriors marking them as Jewish spaces, from the 1840s on, Jews went on a kind of synagogue-building spree. Where they opted, after that date, for humble structures, they did so as a result of the state of their finances and not because they feared displaying their religious distinctiveness on the streets of their towns and cities. After the 1840s they never hesitated to paint or chisel Hebrew letters, along with English ones, announcing the presence of Beth Israel, Tifereth Israel, Kenesseth Israel, Adas Israel, B'nai Israel, Shearith Israel, and a multitude of other Hebrew names, clearly announcing to whoever walked by that the men and women who used this space functioned religiously outside of the Christian tradition; but, like other Americans, they worshiped.

In large cities with multiple congregations, differentiated by class, the better-off congregations opted for grand, soaring structures, which in places like San Francisco and Cincinnati, for example, towered above so

---

28. Irving I. Katz, *110 Years of Temple Beth El Detroit, 1850–1960* (Detroit, MI: Temple Beth El, 1960), n.p.

29. Martin Garfinkle, *The Jewish Community of Washington, D.C.* (Charleston: Arcadia Publishing, 2005), 13.

many of the other buildings on the urban skyline. Additionally, by the latter part of the nineteenth century, even as Americans debated passage of the Christian Nation Amendment, large numbers of Jewish congregations decided to build in an ornate, Moorish style, designed to evoke the Levant, a decidedly un-American, non-European part of the world.

Beyond synagogue buildings, we might also contemplate the perhaps not-notable fact that wherever they lived in America, from the middle of the nineteenth century onward, Jewish merchants put notices in community newspapers and signs on the doors of their stores announcing that these places of business would shutter for their Jewish holidays, Rosh Hashanah, Yom Kippur, and Passover. These owners of clothing stores and dry-goods shops, of men's furnishings or whatever, eager to make a living, concerned about their bottom lines and wanting to establish cordial relations with their non-Jewish customers, felt, it seems, comfortable sharing with the Christian public that they, some times during the year, followed a sacred calendar of their own.

How and why did this happen? How did their religion, something that for most of their long and painful history had been the source of the Jews' suffering and oppression, come in America to be a positive force that fostered the warm greeting they received from the majority Christian population?

On one level, it could have been, given the deeply religious Christian core of American life, that the Jews' Judaism, which inherently meant their rejection of Christianity as a better religion, should have caused them to be rejected, shunned, and marginalized. In a nation in which some of the colonies traced their origin to Christians seeking to build ideal Christian societies, the practitioners of Judaism should have been outcasts and their religion anathema to public life.

Certainly from the early nineteenth century onward, some American Christians considered that they had much to offer the Jews by helping to make them Christians. That is, the evangelical efforts from the 1820s on, stimulated first by the activities of the Society for the Amelioration of the Jews, picked up as their cause the imperative of helping the Jews see the truth, and bringing them to an acceptance of Jesus as their savior. The relatively unsuccessful efforts of the missionaries inspired a good deal of American Jewish community building, as Jews created a set of institutions, including newspapers, hospitals, schools, among others, to counteract the robust efforts at conversion.

The Christian missionaries who roamed poor Jewish neighborhoods merely exercised their First Amendment rights, and their evangelical zeal cannot be seen as evidence of a broad public rejection or demonization of Judaism. They pressed for no suppression of synagogues, no ban on kosher slaughtering, no interference with Jewish burial practices or circumcision. They did what they did, while Jews planted Judaism in America with nearly no controversy, discussion, or stigmatization of their faith community.[30]

Had Americans feared Judaism and considered it alien to their nation, its fate would have been akin to that endured by Catholics, and, in fact, in thinking about the history of Catholicism in America, we can see one context for the acceptance of the Jews as adherents of a particular religious faith.

To put it quite roughly, Jews benefited from the fact that they were not Catholic. In the primarily Protestant population that dominated America from the colonial period well into the early twentieth century, Jews stood out as a group of religious outsiders but not as individuals who belonged to the dreaded, hated Catholic Church. Jews could, in America, breathe easily in that for much of American history anti-Catholicism functioned as a powerful force in public life, shaping politics and leaving its mark on public institutions. The few examples we have of anti-Judaism, the Stuyvesant narrative or the Connecticut one, persisted briefly, had little impact, and took place in the context of the far harsher treatment of the Roman Catholic Church. Whereas the governor general of New Amsterdam had consigned the Jews to private worship, Catholics could not be there at all.

The American colonies came into being as yet one more chapter in the violent affairs attendant on the Protestant Reformation. The women and men who flocked to the colonies, with the exception of those who went to Maryland, where they soon became a minority, came with the profound hatred of Catholicism seared into them. Catholicism, "the whore of Babylon," the "scarlet lady," and their aversion to it shaped them and their American culture in ways that Judaism could not even match. Britain justified the colonization of the Americas in part to be a ballast against the spread of Catholicism into the new world, and for decades the Protestant–Catholic wars of Europe played themselves out in the British colonies of North America. Americans, nearly all Protestants, reveled in public displays of anti-Catholicism yearly on November 5, Guy Fawkes Day, known more commonly as Pope's Day, when crowds gathered to burn the Vicar of Rome in effigy on one American town green after another. Even the American Revolution can be traced back to anti-Catholic origins. One of the great sins of Parliament, according to the patriots, involved the 1774 Quebec Act, passed in conjunction with what they called "the Intolerable Acts," as punishment for the Boston Tea Party. The Protestant New Englanders railed against what they saw as the British favoring the Catholics just north of the border and infringing on local self-governance in Massachusetts.[31]

---

30. Yaakov Ariel, *Evangelizing the Chosen People: Missions to the Jews in America, 1880–2000* (Chapel Hill: University of North Carolina Press, 2000).

31. For notable studies of anti-Catholic sentiment in American history, see Ray Allen

From the colonial period onward, American Protestants believed that Catholicism had no place in a democratic, egalitarian nation that venerated personal freedom and individual choice. Catholicism embodied everything that they abhorred and feared as threats to liberty. An aggressive strain of anti-"Papism" dominated the public discourse of the Protestant nation and spilled over from the churches to the political realm. One of the country's most successful third parties, the Know-Nothings of the 1850s, made anti-Catholicism a core principle, and with this it enjoyed a brief, but still notable, hour in the political spotlight.[32]

The collapse of the Know-Nothings hardly spelled the end of the toxin of anti-Catholicism in American politics. The 1884 presidential election offered a moment in time when anti-Catholicism again infused national politics, as Dr. Samuel Burchard, addressing the Republic National Convention, declared, "we are Republicans, and don't propose to leave our party and identify ourselves with a party," namely, the Democrats, "whose antecedents have been rum, Romanism, and rebellion."[33] The first and the third of these referred to the general disdain of the Democrats for the temperance movement and the preponderance of white southerners in its ranks, instigators, as it were, of the late "rebellion," the secession. But with regard to the middle term, Burchard hoped to rally his fellow activists for the Grand Old Party around the standard of widespread hatred of Rome. Anti-Catholic talk, both viciously popular and also couched in terms of serious discussion, dogged the 1928 campaign of Al Smith, the first Catholic candidate for president. Whether launched by the Ku Klux Klan or by more reasoned commentators, this discourse pivoted around the premise that as a Catholic, Smith took his orders from Rome, he could make no independent judgments in policy based on the good of the country as a whole, and as such had no place in the White House. He lost, resoundingly. Three decades later, John F. Kennedy, the next Catholic candidate for president, had to face a conclave of Protestant ministers in Houston, Texas, and declare that his Catholicism would never compromise his independence, that his adherence to the church did not trump his patriotism, and that he did not submit to the authority of the pope.

Many of the powerful and popular reform movements of the nineteenth century, including temperance, state investment in public educa-

---

Billington, *The Protestant Crusade, 1800–1860: A Study of the Origins of American Nativism* (Chicago: Quadrangle Books, 1938); and Dale Knobel, *Paddy and the Republic: Ethnicity and National in Antebellum America* (Middletown, CT: Wesleyan University Press, 1986).

32. Tyler Anbinder, *Nativism and Slavery: The Northern Know Nothings and the Politics of the 1850s* (New York: Oxford University Press, 1992).

33. William Prendergast, *The Catholic Voter in American Politics: The Passing of the Democratic Monolith* (Washington, DC: Georgetown University Press, 1999), 76.

tion, calls for clean and good government, among others grew out of fear of the growing population of Catholics, mostly immigrants from Ireland. Horace Mann, the outstanding figure in the public school movement of the mid-nineteenth century considered that common schooling would help wean Catholic children away from the defective and dangerous faith of their parents, and cartoonist Thomas Nast advocated for reform of the civil service by depicting the bishops and other prelates of the Catholic Church emerging from the water, depicted as crocodiles, with menacing jaws open, ready to swallow up American liberty with their treacherous teeth. Charles Loring Brace, considered the founder of the American foster-care movement for orphaned and neglected children, envisioned his orphan trains as vehicles by which Catholic children would be swept up from city streets and placed with Protestant farm families. Here in the good air of rural America, Brace asserted, these sad children would lose their Catholicism and be saved by their transformation.

At various times and places, particularly before the Civil War, priests and nuns, marked in the public eye by their unconventional clerical garb, unconventional in the eyes of the Protestant majority, suffered physical assault on the streets. Mobs burned down Catholic churches and convents and spread lurid tales about the evil, satanic rituals that went on behind closed doors. Talk about the Catholic Church echoed with references to the Inquisition, which Catholic prelates would surely establish on American soil if given a chance.

Catholics, according to American discourse, took their orders directly from their priests, who in turn followed the dictates bellowed from Rome. Decidedly discordant with American values about citizenship, independence, and freedom, Catholics, by contrast, as Protestant ministers, orators, writers, and politicians declared, slavishly followed the orders of a foreign potentate, the pope, and they acted as he told them to. Therefore, Catholics did not behave, whether on personal or political matters, according to their own consciences. A foe of modernity, the Catholic Church could, if allowed to grow untrammeled, roll back the progress that Americans believed to be their national and natural birthright.[34]

The Protestant American fear of Catholicism grew out of roots deeply planted in European history, the tumultuous English experience in particular. It flourished in America as Catholic immigration outpaced all other after the 1850s. The arrival of millions of Irish Catholics, followed by Germans, then Slavic, French-Canadian, Italian, and Mexican, made Roman Catholicism the single largest Christian denomination in America by the beginning of the twentieth century. No Protestant denomination came close, and Americans who feared Catholicism as a foe of liberty and inde-

---

34. Higham, *Strangers in the Land.*

pendence considered that they had much to worry about as the number of Catholics seemed to grow without end.

Judaism, by contrast, while seen sometimes as overly legalistic, perhaps a bit medieval and retrograde, particularly vis-à-vis the status of its women in public ritual, enjoyed a place of respectability in the American setting. Such a demonization of Judaism never took place, and Jews, as practitioners of a non-Christian, non-Protestant religion, experienced no opposition to their institution building. As Jewish peddlers, shopkeepers, laborers, merchants, and traders set up their congregations, no Christians worried about the fate of the nation's basic institutions. After all, their numbers never threatened the strength of the nation's Christian dominance. In most places, even in New York, they existed as a minority and their minority status rendered them harmless.

Because they posed no threat, Americans could engage positively with Judaism. Many found Judaism so exotic that mid-nineteenth-century newspapers ran stories about visits to synagogues, describing the rituals they witnessed, telling their readers about the interior designs of these buildings, showing particular interest in the physical separation of women from men, with the former usually ensconced in a balcony overlooking the sanctuary. They assumed and articulated with a sense of awe that what they saw in front of them in New York or Philadelphia or elsewhere resembled the rites and forms of worship that had been conducted in the Temple in Jerusalem. Abolitionist Lydia Maria Childs sat through Rosh Hashanah services at New York's Shearith Israel and commented in the press that "there is something deeply impressive in this remnant of a scattered people, coming down to us in continuous links through the long vista of recorded time . . . keeping up the ceremonial forms of Abraham, Isaac, and Jacob."[35]

Simon Tuska, born in Hungary, came to the United States in 1850 with his father, who served as the rabbi of Congregation B'rith Kodesh in Rochester, New York. The son, the first Jewish student to attend the University of Rochester and the first alumnus of the institution to publish a book, wrote *A Stranger in the Synagogue* in 1854, a guide for non-Jews curious to know about Jewish religious rituals. Tuska's booklet reflected the respectability of the faith tradition planting itself in America rather than its demonization.

From a negative standpoint, antipathy to Judaism spawned no political movements, nor did its arrival and transplantation into America cause American Christians to redefine public policy in order to lessen Judaism's possible pernicious impact. They did not fear for the fate of Christian-

---

35. As cited in Diner, *Time for Gathering*, 180. Original found in Lee Freedman, "Mrs. Child's Visit to a New York Synagogue in 1841," *Publications of the American Jewish Historical Society* 38.1–4 (1948–1949): 181.

ity when congregations like Tuska's established themselves in Rochester or in Memphis, where he eventually accepted a pulpit after receiving
his ordination at the seminary in Breslau. Synagogue buildings, Jewish
cemeteries, schools, and community centers never had to fend off angry
mobs, and while Americans asked questions about Judaism, like Simon
Tuska's classmates at Syracuse University did, they did so out of curiosity
born of lack of familiarity and not out of hatred and fear as they did about
Catholicism.[36]

Catholics were not the only ones who, as members of a despised
religious institution, inspired political and popular opposition among
Americans, particularly in the nineteenth century. Anti-Mormonism took
a different, but equally violent, course, and demonstrated by contrast how
comfortable a place Judaism acquired for itself, and the ease with which
it did so.

Although a native-born religious community, the followers of Mormonism, which developed in New York State's "burnt over district" in
the 1820s, found themselves expelled from one community after another,
going from New York to Ohio and finally to Missouri. In 1838, after the
followers of its founder, Joseph Smith, had established themselves in Kirk-
land, Missouri, the governor of that state declared that Mormons "must be
treated as enemies," to be either slaughtered or driven away. From Missouri the Mormons moved on to Illinois, where they hoped to create their
Zion, their ideal community, in the town of Nauvoo. Smith's imprison-
ment by the state and his lynching at the hands of a mob bent on destroy-
ing the religious community impelled the Mormons to pick up and leave
once again, this time making their trek westward, to Utah, which shortly
thereafter became part of the expanded territory of the United States as a
result of the 1848 Mexican War. It would take a half century and multiple
pieces of congressional legislation before Utah would be admitted to the
union as a state, largely because of rampant anti-Mormonism, which continued to rile the American public

The antipathy against Mormonism stemmed partly from its early
history of plural marriage, something that revolted Americans. It also
reflected an American understanding that as a religion, Mormonism,
which was rejected as *not* being a form of Christianity, placed far greater
emphasis on community boundaries and discipline than on individual
choice, stripping ordinary members of any voice in personal or church
matters. The image of Mormonism that pervaded American talk emphasized how its leadership operated autocratically rather than democrati-
cally, and that it shrouded itself in secrecy, eschewing involvement with
broad, multireligious coalitions of people of good will. Active conversion-

36. Billington, *Protestant Crusade*, 428–29.

ists, the Mormons threatened, by virtue of their missionary campaigns, to lure away adherents from the real Christian churches, which made up the majority of America's houses of worship. At one of its first conventions, the Republic Party declared the Church of Jesus Christ of Latter-Day Saints to be one of the "twin-relics of barbarism," the other being slavery.[37]

By every measure, particularly when compared to the histories of Catholicism and Mormonism, Judaism's path in America proceeded apace from begrudging toleration to acceptance as a partner and player in the nation's religious life. No public reaction marred the Jews' settlement in Ohio, Illinois, and Missouri, nor did their establishment of synagogues and cemetery land launch outbreaks of violence, as did Mormonism. Jews fanned out across the country to pursue economic promise, not because of expulsions and persecutions. Even those who showed up in Utah did so because they saw a market for their wares and not fleeing angry mobs on the other side of the Rocky Mountains.

Despite its clear foreignness and association with an immigrant population, Judaism found for itself a legitimate space on the American religious landscape. Despite its *halakhic,* or legal, underpinning, it managed to portray itself to the American public as a religion of democracy, personal choice, and individualism. Despite its clearly not being Christian, it managed to tame the intensely evangelical nature of American Protestantism and to render the Protestantism that pervaded the public sphere benign and vaguely nondenominational.

How Jews themselves helped bring about this progressive history as they embarked on a reform of their own religious system and as they influenced the public portrayal of their religion deserves a book of its own. Such a book would not only look at the flowering of multiple denominations within American Judaism. It would explore how Jews carefully and successfully presented themselves to their American neighbors as primarily a faith community, as a religion, downplaying the intensely national or ethnic foundation of Jewishness. It would also explicate the historic arguments Jews, rabbis, writers, and thinkers made about their own religion as democratic and as perfectly appropriate to modernity, to America, and to the principle of individual choice. Such a book would in addition look at the role of Jews in refashioning American culture so that it would work for them and their religion, thinking about individuals as diverse as Horace Kallen, who articulated the idea of cultural pluralism, and Irving Berlin, who gave Americans one of their most patriotic of hymns, "God Bless America," which called upon a generic divine being whom anyone, perhaps committed atheists excepted, could sing to as protector of the "land that I love."

---

37. Patrick Mason, *The Mormon Menace: Violence and Anti-Mormonism in the Postbellum South* (Oxford: Oxford University Press, 2011), 81.

But answering the question of how America met the Jews in the religious sphere directs our attention away from the Jews themselves, in terms of the kinds of communities they built and the kinds of religious practices and forms they opted for, to a focus on America. It met the Jews in the context of its overarching valorization of religion, in part because it had decoupled matters of faith from state power, allowing the latter to be embraced as a positive force for promoting civic virtue. While historians of the American Jewish experience may debate the degree to which the veneration of religion in America pushed Jews to repackage themselves as a "faith community" as opposed to a people or a nation, the prevailing positive view of religion in America allowed Jews to argue for extending to their religion the benefits that all other denominations enjoyed because all religions engaged in good work. By being bound to one another through a "religion," a concept somewhat extraneous to normative Judaism, American Jews could stand under the protective umbrella of American culture.

America also met the Jews as a nation that adopted into its Constitution the principle of separation of church and state, declaring in the First Amendment that Congress could not sanction any religion over any other, but it could do nothing to prevent Americans from exercising freely their religious beliefs. Obviously the complicated history of these two halves of the amendment has been the subject of vast scholarly and legal analysis and debate. While many gray areas, such as Sunday closings, vexed Jews along with Seventh Day Adventists, most aspects of public life fell clearly into one zone or the other, state versus religion, public versus private.

Even so simple a fact as the state not collecting statistics on who belonged to what denomination, if they belonged at all, meant that private beliefs, matters of the spirit, did not require public declarations. Immigrants may have been classified by color and race, but their religions did not interest government officials. No check-off boxes on census forms or on tax statements demanded or suggested that individuals divulge to the government officials their religious affiliation. Tax monies did not pay the salaries of the clergy. Rather, despite their learning and their ordination, clergy had to go hat in hand to their congregants for their financial support, transforming ordinary members into the equivalent of "we, the people" who exercised the power to "ordain and establish this Constitution for the United States of America."

Finally, as America met the Jews and provided a comfortable space for their religion, it got an opportunity to distinguish itself from Europe, the place back there, which everyone, African Americans and native peoples excepted, left because of its narrowness. So much of nineteenth- and twentieth-century American vernacular culture got framed around a series of rhetorical binaries, pitting old, aristocratic, class-ridden Europe against democratic America with freedom for all, bristling with newness. After all, Emma Lazarus invoked in her "New Colossus" the Europe–

America juxtaposition of "Keep ancient lands, your storied pomp" with the welcoming open "golden door." When Jewish notables gathered on Thanksgiving Day 1905, at New York's Carnegie Hall, along with former president Grover Cleveland, Frank Higgins, the governor of New York State, as well as other non-Jewish political and religious elites, they emphasized in their speeches in celebration of 250 years of Jewish life in America how America differed from Europe, Russia in particular, where the largest number of Jews lived. There, "the Eastern land of tyranny and destruction," in the words of Rabbi Joseph Silverman of New York's Temple Emanuel, "our suffering brethren . . . are passing through the fire that commeth and the water that overwhelmeth." But in America, "we have established our habitations and tabernacles, here we have erected our synagogues and homes for the needy, the orphans and widows, the sick and forlorn."[38]

Within the florid language, Silverman made a crucial point. The fact that America extended an open hand to Judaism provided yet one more way it could distinguish itself from Europe, the hotbed of anti-Semitism, home of the Inquisition, the ghettoes, the pogroms, the Jew badges, and the generalized persecution of the Jews. American Protestants could congratulate themselves and their nation for the relatively untroubled and uncomplicated way in which they received the Jews, women and men whom they anointed as pilgrims, fleeing religious persecution. Europe hounded the Jews, they argued, patting themselves on their metaphoric collective shoulders, while America provided the Jews with unrestricted opportunities to worship as they pleased. Silverman's emphasis that America's goodness made possible the Jews' synagogues, "tabernacles," and social service institutions put religion front and center of their presentation of themselves in the American context.

In these multiple ways, religion and the broad context of religious life in America worked for the Jews. Ironically in their long history, stretching back many centuries, their religion had set them apart from others, marginalized them from the dominant population, whatever its particular religion, and served as the basis for their sufferings. Religion provided the badge of their difference, the core of what it meant to be an outsider. It restricted where they could live and how they could make a living, defining them as problems to be contended with in their Christian and Muslim states.

Elsewhere religion handicapped the Jews, but in America it helped them. Despite the overwhelming Christian majority population and the inescapable Protestant public culture, the state made Judaism an active

---

38. *The Two Hundred and Fiftieth Anniversary of the Settlement of the Jews in the United States: Addresses Delivered at Carnegie Hall, New York, on Thanksgiving Day MCMV* (New York: New York Cooperative Society, 1905), 6–7.

partner in enhancing civic life. In America their religion provided them with a point of entry into the common culture, showing it off as something that ennobled them and that made their community life consistent with the nation's self-image as a nation of worshipers.

Jews had much to gain from the fact that Americans saw them as religious refugees fleeing Europe's bigotry and persecution. Particularly starting in the 1890s, as some Americans began to call for government limitations on immigration, Jews had little difficulty presenting themselves as primarily the victims of religious violence in Europe, galvanized by the religious freedom available to them in America.

Yet ironically the great Jewish immigration to the United States reflected much more the workings of more prosaic economic forces, and while surely not denying the intensity of the hatreds heaped on them in Europe, the movement to America took place in the close relationship between the economic limitations Jews experienced in Europe and the particular conditions of life in America, which like mass immigration, the privileging of whiteness, and the power of religion defined as a force for good, greeted them upon their arrival.

4

More than Bread and More than Roses: Jews in the Land of Materialism

Historian David Shi offered a suggestive proposition in his book *The Simple Life* (1985), which provides yet another direction in which to steer this exploration of how America met the Jews, though he said nothing directly about Jews, Judaism, their migrations to America, or the ways by which they interacted in their new home with their non-Jewish neighbors. "The tension between accumulating goods," he declared in his first chapter, "and cultivating goodness appeared early in the American experience and has lingered long." [1] *The Simple Life*, cast primarily as an intellectual history, sought to prove that throughout American history, from the age of the Puritans through the 1980s, some Americans organized their lives to cultivate "goodness" by eschewing material consumption, having striven to do with less, to acquire fewer goods than they could afford, purchasing only what they needed. Shi analyzes the words and ideas of a number of intellectuals and religious thinkers who forcefully condemned acquisitiveness and the ethos of more is better, that a person's worth might be gauged by what he or she bought and displayed.

Those Americans, the advocates and practitioners of the "simple life," the book demonstrated, organized their lives differently from most Americans around them and did so consciously and in striking opposition to a basic element in American life, namely, the celebration of consumption, the desire to have more and more things. Had Shi's subjects been the national outliers, had enthusiastic consumption not been the norm, America might not have been so attractive a destination for Europe's Jews, and the meeting between the Jews and the Americans who greeted them may not have gone so well.

Rather, the America to which the Jews streamed and where they succeeded so well might be best thought of in the words of the nineteenth-century economist Thorstein Veblen as a place motivated by the impulse

---

1. David Shi, *The Simple Life: Plain Living and High Thinking in American Culture* (New York: Oxford University Press, 1985), 8.

of "conspicuous consumption."[2] The Americans likewise can be thought of in terms of an expression coined by historian David Potter in his 1954 national character study as a "people of plenty."

Potter traced the veneration and the reality of widespread American acquisition to its material abundance. That abundance of resources, particularly land, and everything in and on it, minerals, forests, water, and animals, gave a distinctive cast to American life back to the colonial era. He quoted a play produced in England in 1605, aptly entitled *Eastward Ho*, as an example of it, both in terms of image and actuality, as one character carried on, declaiming, "Gold is more plentiful there than copper is with us," while a second one countered with the more quotidian, "As ever the sun shined on: temperate and all sorts of excellent viands; wild boar there is as common as our tamest bacon is here, and venison as mutton."[3]

After all, the British, French, Spanish, Dutch, and even Swedes wanted all or parts of America because of the fur on the backs of beaver running wild, the trees in seemingly limitless profusion, and the land for farming, which required only the exile or extirpation of the inhabitants defined as savages and as such outside the definition of humanity.

Potter, writing in the aftermath of World War II and the victory of the free nations of the world, mostly the United States and Britain, over the forces of fascism and Nazism, and during the Cold War, which pitted American capitalism against Soviet communism, attributed much to that plenty which one might say nature bestowed on America, not the least of which involved the forging of democracy. Democracy, Potter wrote, could not flourish in "a country with inadequate wealth." Democracies like the United States, according to *People of Plenty*, promise plenty to their citizens and by extension those who would become citizens, "stimulating people to demand" and affording opportunity to acquire more than a "meager living."[4]

That connection between the demand for goods, for lives lived beyond the "meager living," and mass democracy, and the ways in which that quest for consumption dominated American life surfaced boldly in Tocqueville's writings as well. On this subject he had much to say about a defining characteristic of the new nation. He did not necessarily find it impressive or without a steep price tag affixed, describing how:

> The inhabitant of the United States is attached to the goods of this world as if he were assured of not dying, and he hastens so much to seize those

---

2. Thorstein Veblen, *The Theory of the Leisure Class* (New York: Macmillan, 1899), 64–70.

3. David Potter, *People of Plenty: Economic Abundance and the American Character* (Chicago: University of Chicago Press, 154), 78.

4. Ibid., 113.

goods that pass within his reach, that you would say that at every instant that he is afraid of ceasing to live before enjoying them. He seizes all of them, but without gripping them, and he soon lets them escape from his hands in order to run after new enjoyments.[5]

Tocqueville's trove of observations on American materialism continued as he mused that "You are at first astounded contemplating this singular agitation exhibited by so many happy men, in the very midst of abundance. This spectacle is, however, as old as the world; what is new is that we see it presented by an entire people." Americans living in the 1830s, in Tocqueville's eyes, experienced displeasure and fear because of their unquenchable pursuit of earthly goods, which many worried they would not be able to acquire. This dissatisfaction despite abundance emerged as a typical and prevalent trait Tocqueville assigned to the population of this relatively new republic.[6]

Not that Tocqueville, Veblen, Potter, or generations of historians, creative writers, anthropologists, sociologists, and economists denied the existence of poverty in America or the vast discrepancies between the well-off and the poor, the gaping chasm between the haves and the have-nots. Rather, they argued that despite the reality that throughout American history class inequities existed, that those who had much wanted to have more and those who had least, struggled and suffered in order to get more. The *desire* to acquire goods united the classes, and consumption, actual or aspirational, linked the top and the bottom of the economic and social ladder.

Americans' widespread yearning for things material, including but hardly limited to more houses and bigger vehicles, closets crammed with jewelry, watches, and clothing, homes furnished with tables and chairs, beds, shelves, mirrors, and linens, as well as tables sagging with food in abundance, made America, in the words of the historian Elizabeth Ewen, "the land of dollars."[7] That land that existed in the imaginary realm as a place where anyone with just enough grit and determination could rise above wherever he started—nearly always cast in male terms, with some exceptions—helped shape a further aspect of America's attractiveness for Europe's Jewish masses looking for new homes.

American culture, portrayed in textbooks, the press, and fiction, in sermons, on the stage, and in celluloid on the silver screen, venerated the so-called self-made man. A construct circumscribed by race and gender and essentially limited to white men, the ethos of the scrappy up-start

---

5. Tocqueville, *Democracy in America*, 943–44.

6. Ibid., 944.

7. Elizabeth Ewen, *Immigrant Women in the Land of Dollars: Life and Culture on the Lower East Side, 1890–1925* (New York: Monthly Review Press, 1985).

who by dint of his own efforts moved from rags to riches, from poverty to wealth, extended back to the writings of Benjamin Franklin in his *Autobiography* and continued undimmed well into the twentieth century as real figures such as Henry Ford, Thomas Edison, Andrew Carnegie, and a cast of characters, all poor white boys who ended up as fabulously wealthy men, fueled the scramble for riches.

The late nineteenth-century Baptist preacher Russell Herman Conwell delivered his "Acres of Diamonds" speech over six thousand times, traveling throughout the country and the world, advising his listeners, no matter how humble their circumstances, "You ought to be rich," and reminding them that "money is power." Conwell served as an apostle for American fantasies of economic mobility and the value of wealth to enhance life and further consumption.[8]

Few, very few, individuals, even those with the correct phenotype, ever even approximated this ideal, as sketched out in the writings of the nineteenth-century popular writer Horatio Alger in the figures of Ragged Dick and other scrappy protagonists. (Alger would serve as a private tutor in the home of one Jewish immigrant to America, Joseph Seligman, who went from being a peddler in the Pennsylvania anthracite coal region to a millionaire banker, an embodiment of the mythic American narrative.)[9]

These twinned phenomena, the love of material consumption and the lionization of the rich man who started out poor, deeply informed American public culture, creating an ethos that pervaded the educational, political, and religious life of the nation. It had far-reaching consequences, well beyond the scope of this short book. But as an idea, even as a delusion, it has distinguished America from most other places in the world, particularly those from which immigrants came. It served as the most magnetic of draws to America.

Most immigrants, not just Europeans, left places of low productivity, attracted to America's economic possibilities. No naïfs, they did not believe that gold beckoned to them from the cobblestones of its streets nor did they consider as anything other than amusing the words of the nineteenth-century Norwegian folk song, written by Ole Bull as he mythologized America:

> In Oleanna, land is free,
> The wheat and corn just plant themselves,
> Then grow a good four feet a day,
> While on your bed you rest yourself.

---

8. Russell Herman Conwell, *Acres of Diamonds* (New York: Harper & Bros., 1915), 17–22.

9. John Cawelti, *Apostles of the Self-Made Man* (Chicago: University of Chicago Press, 1988); Irvin G. Wyllie, *The Self-Made Man in America: The Myth of from Rags to Riches* (Houston, TX: Free Press, 1966).

Little roasted piggies
just rush around the city streets,
Inquiring so politely if
A slice of ham you'd like to eat.

But Bull's final verse did in fact accurately reflect something of the wide-spread ideas that circulated in Europe and elsewhere about America, its opportunities for those struggling economically back home, as he wrote that for "the poorest wretch in Norway," Oleanna—America—offered possibilities for consumption.[10] Eating better, having more clothes, living in a more commodious dwelling place, and furnishing it with this and that constituted immigrant standards of success. Historian Ewa Morawska captured the material aspirations of Slavic steelworkers and miners in Johnstown, Pennsylvania, in her well-titled *For Bread with Butter*. In spite of their exploitation in the mills and mines and all the dangers they faced in their workplaces, they, in fact, did get, for the first time in their lives, to eat bread with butter on a regular basis, live in markedly more commo-dious homes, which they furnished more elaborately than they had their dwelling places back home.[11]

New Americans and those with deep, multigenerational roots in the United States across racial, ethnic, and religious lines, urban and rural, engaged with the bounty of goods available to them and aspired to have more. Historians who have studied this culture of consumption and com-mentators, religious and political, over the course of several centuries, including those who celebrated it and those who bemoaned it, have con-verged on an understanding that Americans understood themselves as consumers.

The American engagement with consumerism shaped much of the nation's culture and cannot be disconnected from nearly any national developments. This love of material goods and the belief that more stuff leads to a better life reflected and conjoined with a culture of modernity, individualism, and a faith in, and assumption of, the inevitability of prog-ress. While other peoples in other places no doubt also enjoyed warm blankets, ticking clocks, shiny jewelry, thick carpets, fast cars, shiny refrig-erators, and the like, none who have analyzed American life have failed to comment on the love of all these good things manifested by Americans and the fact that more Americans had access to them than did their coun-terparts in other countries and continents.[12]

---

10. Theodore Blegen and Martin Ruuds, eds., *Norwegian Emigrant Songs and Ballads* (Minneapolis: University of Minnesota Press, 1936), 282–83.

11. Ewa Morawska, *For Bread with Butter: The Life-Worlds of East Central Europeans in Johnstown, Pennsylvania, 1890–1940* (New York: Cambridge University Press, 1985).

12. A very important new book makes this point in detail. See Frank Trentmann, *Empire*

No tradition of antimaterialism influenced public life, and David Shi's subjects in *The Simple Life* held little sway over the farmers and workers, the rural dwellers and city folk, the families who moved out to the frontier and those who bought homes in the suburbs that came to ring the urban cores. Immigrants and "real" Americans, whites and African Americans, managers and laborers, shared an orientation that acquiring material goods would make them feel good, successful, and invested in the stability of society. Conversely, not being able to consume marked them as failures, in their own eyes and those of others.

Historian Lisabeth Cohen, writing about the post–World War II era, described America as a "consumer's republic," but her expression could easily fit earlier periods as well, as a nation that "derived its inner strength from the access ordinary women and men had to the goods that they wanted." Yet another historian, Susan Matt, writing about the late nineteenth and early twentieth centuries, referred to an ethos of "material democracy," highlighting an advertisement from the Phoenix Hosiery Company of 1922 that announced boldly, "Democracy! All America has come into the silk stocking class," as it touted its product that had brought "hosiery elegance with the reach of all."[13]

In the most fundamental sense, this materialism, like the American obsession with skin color and the valorization of religion, had nothing to do with Jews, whether in their early years as immigrants or in the lives of their American-born children and grandchildren. As a defining element of American culture it predated their arrival, existed as an independent force in the life of the nation, and would have shaped the public culture if no or few Jews had chosen America over all the other places to which they could have gone.

But yet this love of materialism and the popular adulation of the self-made man (again I use the gendered term because Americans used it, and it reflected ideas about American masculinity) had much to do with causing Jews to opt for America, and they help us understand the positive greeting that awaited the Jews on this side of the Atlantic.

The massive transfer of Jewish population to America drew millions of Jews from places of low productivity and stagnant development to the most dynamic economy in the world, and in that national setting of constantly expanding possibilities, Jews not only improved their own lot but brought to Americans exactly what they wanted.

---

of Things: How We Became a World of Consumers, from the Fifteenth Century to the Twenty-First (New York: Harper, 2016).

13. Lizabeth Cohen, *A Consumers Republic: The Politics of Mass Consumption in Postwar America* (New York: Vintage Books, 2003); Susan Matt, *Keeping Up with the Joneses: Envy in American Consumer Culture, 1890–1930* (Philadelphia: University of Pennsylvania Press, 2003), 25.

This history of how America met the Jews cannot be disassociated from the long, global history of Jews and commerce.[14] For centuries, or longer, Jews served as the bearers of goods, carrying items from one market to another, from producers to consumers, from cities to peasants and rural dwellers. Historians have documented how Jews at the beginning of the Common Era followed the Roman armies into Europe, for example, serving as traders who shuttled between the far provinces in Gaul and Spain and the metropolis. The Mediterranean served as not just a "Roman Lake" but a Jewish one as well, as Jewish merchants sailed around its basin carrying finished products, fabrics, gold, or whatever goods could yield a profit. They also penetrated the hinterlands, establishing communities that facilitated trade, and they conducted business among themselves and also sold to broad and diverse publics. Trade propelled Jews along the Silk Road into central Asia. It brought them to eastern Europe, as they migrated from the west starting in approximately the year 1000, and their commercial enterprises helped to spread them throughout the Ottoman Empire and all over North Africa.

The answer to the question of how and why Jews opted for trade over the course of so many centuries not only lies far beyond this interpretive essay or my ken but also, no doubt, has no one definitive answer. Too big a subject to even try to encapsulate here, it touches on a number of key themes that do flow into the history of how America greeted the Jews. Trade solidified Jewish communal bonds. Its portability allowed women and men with no rights of residence to be able to pick up and start over someplace else, someplace that wanted the goods that Jews purveyed. Trade made it possible for them to scope out new and better opportunities in whatever novel setting they learned about and could get to, still carrying on their familiar operations, continuing to rely upon well-developed networks. Commerce provided a meeting point between Jews, with their separate communal structures and distinctive religion, and the Christians or Muslims or others with whom they traded and among whom they lived.[15]

For Jews in most places other than the United States, Jewish involvement with trade functioned as something of a double-edged sword. While the buying and selling of goods brought them to, for example, Poland in

---

14. What follows is not intended as a full, in-depth history of Jews in the American economy. That clearly would require much more space, an exploration of the vast literature on the subject, and a different kind of analysis.

15. Rebecca Kobrin and Adam Teller, *Purchasing Power: The Economics of Modern Jewish History* (Philadelphia: University of Pennsylvania Press, 2016), provides a wide range of essays on this subject, covering for the modern period almost the entirety of the Jewish diaspora. For a monograph of Jewish involvement in the modern economy, see Derek Penslar, *Shylock's Children: Economics and Jewish Identity in Modern Europe* (Berkeley: University of California Press, 2001).

the Middle Ages and provided them with a way to make a living, and for some a very handsome one at that, it also made them markedly different from all the people around them, Christians, who mainly labored as agricultural peasants and who for centuries had been legally tied to the land and the nobles who owned it. Jewish trade operated in the middle between the peasants and the landowners, often employed by the landowners in a variety of commercial capacities. Resented by the poor exploited peasants as the agents of the nobility, the Jews, as the bearers of sundry goods and buyers of agricultural products, occupied an unenviable position. Their business dealings exacerbated their already fraught otherness in this deeply Christian society.

As the Jews lived there only on the sufferance of the landowners, they had to do the bidding of the powerful. Part of that bidding involved buying up the grains or other crops at the lowest cost and selling goods at the highest, hardly a formula to win over and develop positive relationships with the peasantry. If the peasants, however, failed in producing their crops, the burden fell on the Jews—hardly a formula to maintain smooth relations with those in power.[16]

This very brief description of Poland could equally fit Alsace, Bohemia, Bavaria, and most any other place in Europe, where so many Jews made a living in trade, but wherein that trade bred animosity between them and their non-Jewish neighbors. In general, Jews tended to have more positive interactions with Protestant customers than with Catholics, and Catholic societies exhibited a more decidedly suspicious outlook on issues of consumption and credit. In the few Catholic-migration destinations that attracted Jews, namely, Ireland, Quebec, and Latin America, they met greater animosity and endured more in the way of organized protests based on their trade than they did in the Protestant ones, the United States, Great Britain, English-speaking Canada, Australia, and South Africa.[17]

None of this prevailed in America. While most Americans until the late nineteenth century made their living in farming, they did so in a very different way from their European counterparts. Most white farmers owned their own land, and although large-scale enterprises came to dominate by the early twentieth century, Jews did not function as the middle-men agents of any ruling class of landowners, hated by the toilers on the land. Even in the American South, the land of sharecroppers and tenant farmers, and in mining communities, Jewish peddlers, key players in the meeting between America and the Jews, did not work for the owners of the land or the mine operators. They worked for themselves or for Jewish shopkeepers and as such did not represent the forces of exploitation in the

---

16. Gershon Hundert, *The Jews in a Polish Private Town: The Case of Opatów in the Eighteenth Century* (Baltimore, MD: Johns Hopkins University Press, 1992).

17. Diner, *Roads Taken*.

lives of the exploited. Indeed, Jewish peddlers and storekeepers provided rural African Americans, coal miners in Appalachia and elsewhere, and poor white laborers in textile-mill towns alternative sources of goods to the hated company stores, operated and owned by the same employers whom they despised.

Part of the explanation of the economic role of the Jews in America and the positive energy it generated lies in the phenomenon of widespread landowning, the existence of an ever-expanding frontier of land, stolen from the native peoples, and the ability of most white Americans to experience some degree of economic satisfaction, particularly in terms of expanded opportunities for material consumption. These overarching forces provided a relatively infertile soil for the flourishing of the kind of economic resentment that pulsated through European society against the Jews.

Not that such economically charged anti-Jewish sentiment from below never flared in the United States, but it did so sporadically; and when it did, it paled in comparison to the acceptance Jews as individuals experienced because of their economic roles. In the late nineteenth century, for example, in the midst of an agricultural crisis that spawned populist outpourings in parts of the Midwest and the South, some advocates for farmer militancy seized on the image of the Jewish bankers and the manipulators of currency as the cause of the farmers' distress.

Georgia, for example, holds a place of distinction in the annals of American Jewish history as the place where Leo Frank died at the hands of an enraged lynch mob, after having undergone a number of trials, all laced with anti-Semitic discourse in the courtroom and in the public sphere, the press in particular. Yet a post-Civil War era Atlanta newspaper, just a few decades before the murderous actions, declaimed how much it hoped to see an influx of Jews to boost the state's business profile. "We congratulate ourselves," the editor wrote, "because nothing is so indicative of a city's progress as to see an influx of Jews who come with the intention of living with you and especially as they buy property and build among you because they are a thrifty and progressive people."[18]

The welcoming rhetoric that pivoted around the idea of Jews as the conveyors of wanted goods and the catalysts for local prosperity existed, for sure, alongside words about Jews as desecraters of the nation's Christian core values. Some Christian conservatives considered that Jewish department-store owners perverted the true meaning of Christmas with their lavish window displays of gifts for adults and children, rendering the holiday less about the birth of the baby Jesus and more about iceskates, sleds, new dresses, layaway plans, and Christmas clubs to facilitate

---

18. Quoted in Diner, *Time for Gathering,* 169.

the buying of all sorts of material objects for both the "naughty" and the "nice," as intoned in the popular song "Santa Claus Is Coming to Town," first performed in 1934 on Eddie Cantor's radio show. That Jews wrote, produced, and broadcast some of the most popular, nonreligious, gift-oriented Christmas songs, like "Rudolph the Red-Nose Reindeer," probably the most beloved of all the seasonal songs celebrating the material aspect of the American holiday, only confirmed the worst assessments offered by deeply faithful Christians who considered that Jews preyed upon Americans' weakness for gaudy things and in the process sapped away at America's true Christian culture.[19]

Such rhetoric led to nearly no action against Jews, and in the same states and counties where such words could be heard, Jewish shopkeepers and Jewish peddlers continued to interact positively with their customers, experiencing no threats of physical violence or economic reprisal.[20] Even when disgruntled farmers in Kansas or Georgia, or poor city dwellers in New York or Chicago railed against "the Jews" as the cause of their economic miseries, Jews enjoyed the full bundle of state-endowed rights, undisturbed by the possibility that those with power would decide that the Jews were a liability. They never had to worry that they would be expelled from their communities or would suffer a diminution of the fundamental privileges that came to them as citizens. They knew that they were not just tolerated guests, like their ancestors had been in their various former places of residence, and indeed as some of their peers still experienced in, say, Poland or Lithuania. For the most part, economically driven anti-Jewish arguments remained on the margins of American life, and most Americans did not see Jews as the source of economic distress or class disparities. Jews rather as neighbors sold them the goods they wanted, and the customers appreciated the chance to consume.

To understand the meeting between America and the Jews, we might keep in mind that from its earliest days until well into the twentieth century America experienced a constant and chronic labor shortage, set amid the vast natural resources waiting to be exploited. This reality undergirded the entire European immigrant flood to America, that of the Jews as well. The Jewish migration, similar to nearly all others, has to be thought of as

---

19. For more on Jewish composers of Christmas music, see chapter 4 of Joshua Plaut, *A Kosher Christmas: 'Tis the Season to be Jewish* (New Brunswick, NJ: Rutgers University Press, 2012).

20. Richard Hofstadter first argued for the connection in Richard Hofstadter, *The Age of Reform: From Bryan to F.D.R.* (New York: Vintage Books, 1955), 70–82. Walter Nugent challenged the writings of scholars like Hofstadter who linked populism to anti-Semitism; see Walter Nugent, *The Tolerant Populists: Kansas, Populism and Nativism* (Chicago: University of Chicago Press, 1963), ix–x. Norman Pollack also challenged Hofstadter's linkage of populism and anti-Semitism; see Norman Pollack, "Hofstadter on Populism: A Critique of the Age of Reform," *Journal of Southern History* 26 (1960): 478–500.

a labor migration, as a movement of people in search of work, pushed out by the limited possibilities for work at home and pulled by the knowledge of such possibilities in the destination.

Like all other immigrants, Jews left settled places where economic opportunities did not exist for them and opted for America where they did. Perhaps better put, chances for making a living back home did exist but not in large-enough numbers for the population of relatively poor young people, the typical immigrants, in search of a livelihood. In central Europe in the mid-nineteenth century, young Jews with some capital at their command and who knew the German language flocked to cities such as Berlin and Vienna and entered into the world of commerce. Those, however, with little or no capital, and who still spoke exclusively the Jewish vernacular, Judeo-German, made their way instead across the Atlantic.

The tight nexus between Jews and commerce helped in stimulating their orientation toward the United States, their arrival, settlement, diffusion, and integration into the country. Not that all Jewish immigrants who arrived in America did so in order to buy and sell something. Certainly after the 1870s, the largest number, hundreds of thousands of women and men, took their first American steps into the garment industry as relatively unskilled low-wage laborers; but given the fact that nearly all of them worked for Jewish employers, the economic fate of the Jewish working class reflected and grew out of the business activities of their coreligionist bosses.

The Jews' move to America, a place wedded to the celebration of material consumption, takes us to the large and complex history of capitalism, as the economic system most intimately associated with modernity, and to the history of the United States, a nation that historians have declared to have been born modern. The lack of a feudal past, individualism as a social ideal, equality in the eyes of the state, and the freedom of white people to pursue whatever occupations they wanted, and to live, worship, and consume as they preferred structured American life and made the nation a hospitable environment for free enterprise, the accumulation of capital, without governmental interference in the affairs of business.

Tens of thousands of Jewish men opted for the United States and began their lives there as itinerant peddlers, going from house to house, farm to farm, selling goods from packs on their backs. The fact that at no time and in no place did the state impede their ability, as white people, to traverse the roads, to go wherever they considered they might find paying customers, made a difference.

The German sociologist Max Weber considered that the Protestant Reformation catalyzed the rise of capitalism and as such the birth of modernity, but another German sociologist, Werner Sombart, posited that the Jews, with their extensive history of trade, their religious proclivities, their exclusion from agriculture, and their inherent racial characteristics, served as the engines of capitalism.

Neither thinker can be definitively proved right or wrong (other than Sombart for falsely insisting on race as a real, fixed, and an innate life force) in terms of solving the riddle as to who made capitalism possible. But in what might seem a kind of perfect fit, or at least a historical kind of serendipity, the Jews, a group of people whose history had been shaped by trade, whose historic migrations had for millennia followed trade routes, made their way to this most Protestant of nations and took off because of the vast resources it contained, ready for use by and for capitalism.

The American Jewish communal narrative has focused on European anti-Semitism as the cause of the migration. In particular, it has highlighted a dramatic tale in which outbreaks of anti-Jewish violence, the pogroms in particular, usually dated as having begun in 1881, served as the engines that drove the population transfer. This rendition of the past served all sorts of purposes, including distinguishing Jews from other immigrants who supposedly chose America purely for economic reasons; analytically the more ordinary and mundane story works with the available data. Jews, like their co-immigrants in steerage, as well as those who came earlier from places such as Ireland and those who came later such as those from Mexico, sought out new places to live better than they could at home, aspiring to ultimately live well.

The Nobel Prize–winning economist Simon Kuznets, among others, handily overturned the pogrom narrative and the idea that the Jewish masses from the Russian Empire, those whose arrival contributed the largest number to the American Jewish population, made their way to the United States in desperate flight from life-threatening violence. Kuznets set data collected at Ellis Island, the largest of the U.S. immigrant-receiving stations, which opened in 1892, against the data collected in 1902 by the Jewish Colonization Association in the Pale of Settlement and showed conclusively the selectivity of the emigrants from the Russian Empire and the immigrants to America in terms of region, class, age, marital status, and occupation, making it clear that going to America involved a careful process of decision making and that it appealed to some Jews, not others.[21]

Even without Kuznets's empirical evidence, the economic draw of America should have been clear by looking at patterns of Jewish migration from the Czarist lands after the 1880s. Not only did the first decades of eastern European Jewish immigrants hail primarily from Lithuania, the most overpopulated, poorest region and the one where the pogroms did not flare, but so many also emigrated from Galicia and other parts of the Austro-Hungarian Empire, where they endured poverty but not

---

21. Kuznets, "Immigration of Russian Jews," 35–124.

brutal violence. Additionally, among the post-1870s Jewish immigrants, married men typically left home first, with their older children, able-bodied workers, in tow, and got themselves launched in America either as garment workers, as laborers in some other industry, or in some kind of business. They then called for wives and younger children, and at times parents, when they had saved enough money to pay for steamship tickets and could afford to provide a livable home. Had the migration actually been an immediate and pressing response to violence, wives and small children, the elderly as well, would hardly have been expected to face the mobs on their own.

Rather, the eastern European Jewish immigrants of the 1870s through the 1920s, like those who arrived earlier in the nineteenth century, primarily from central Europe and even those who showed up in America as far back as the prenational period, had making a living on their minds. In every period of American Jewish history, with the exception of Jewish migration from Nazi-dominated Europe in the 1930s, we can see a confluence between American material needs, or better wants, and Jewish economic experiences, fostering a symbiotic relationship between the two. Reasonable economic prospects facilitated their meeting.

That symbiotic relationship not only drew Jews to America but created the mutually beneficial context that stimulated further Jewish immigration and fostered Jewish integration. Not that all Jews did well, or that none endured poverty over an extended period of time. Economic distress always existed among Jews in America, whether immigrants or their descendants. The communities they built existed in large measure as venues to aid the poor, whether orphans, widows, the aged, the sick, or those who just could not make it in the harsh world of American capitalism. Jewish philanthropists devised a bevy of schemes to alleviate poverty and lessen immigrant unemployment, like the Industrial Removal Office, founded in 1901, which helped impoverished Jewish men move out of New York, setting them up in jobs in smaller communities in the hinterlands. Other organizations tried to promote Jewish farming, and in one large city after another Jewish aid organizations sought ways to assist the poor.[22]

The positive response of Jewish women and men to the messages of unionization and of socialism also indicated the degree to which so many of them struggled with economic difficulties. Tens of thousands of them turned to mass movements to improve their own economic lot and that of the others who labored in the garment factories and in society as a whole. A substantial number of Jews in America participated in popular and theoretical attacks on capitalism as an evil system that had to

22. Robert Rockaway, *Words of the Uprooted: Jewish Immigrants in Early Twentieth Century America* (Ithaca, NY: Cornell University Press, 1998).

be exposed and replaced because of the poverty that they knew and saw around them.[23]

Nor did a narrative of meteoric economic mobility, a mass Jewish skyrocketing from the bottom of the working class to the top echelons of wealth, actually conform to reality. For most of the immigrants it took a generation or two to make the move out of the ranks of industrial laborers and small-time merchants scraping by, and they moved incrementally, not in one jump upward. The process by which their daughters became teachers and social workers and their sons, lawyers, doctors, accountants, and proprietors of substantial businesses proceeded much more slowly than the mythic tale relates. Even in the twenty-first century, pockets of poverty among Jews persist stubbornly, according to surveys of Jewish communal institutions.[24]

But in the main, the migration did lead to a marked improvement in the economic lot of those Jews who opted for America. As a strategy to improve the lives of families and individuals, it represented a fairly good bet, as women and men weighed and calculated the benefits and liabilities of staying put, moving to some other new home, or sailing for America. On the one hand, Jewish immigrants, once living in the United States, sent tremendous amounts of money in the form of remittances to kin still living back home, as well as contributions to Jewish institutions in Europe, attesting to the immigrants' ability to earn, save, and also finance Jewish life in the "old country." On the other hand, at least one careful study comparing Jewish immigrants from eastern Europe in London with those in New York found that the latter outearned the former and did so substantially through entrepreneurship. These data provide in fact one clue as to why many Jewish immigrants to England considered it not a final destination but a way station to the real prize, the United States.

Jews in England enjoyed the same rights as their American coreligionists in terms of their unmolested right to the observance of Judaism, but the word circulated in the Jewish world, back in eastern Europe and on the streets of London, Manchester, and Leeds, that America offered the best place to make a living, that Americans welcomed Jews as sellers of goods, and that welcome spelled success for new immigrants.

Yet another issue suggests itself in this context, one fraught with mythology, hyperbole, and to a certain degree ethnic chauvinism, namely,

23. Michels, *Fire in Their Hearts*; Rockaway, *Words of the Uprooted*; Ellen Eisenberg, *Jewish Agricultural Colonies in New Jersey: 1882–1920* (Syracuse, NY: Syracuse University Press, 1995).

24. For more on the trend of first-generation American Jewish women entering the teaching profession, see Ruth Markowitz, *My Daughter, the Teacher: Jewish Teachers in New York City Schools* (New Brunswick, NJ: Rutgers University Press, 1993). For more on poverty in the Jewish community, see Sherry Gorelick, *City College and the Jewish Poor: Education in New York, 1880–1924* (New Brunswick, NJ: Rutgers University Press, 1982).

the degree to which Jews experienced more rapid economic mobility than other immigrant groups in the United States. While accurate statistics defy easy gathering and empirical accuracy, and though the data we have vary from place to place, they do point to a quicker sprint upward for the Jews as they went from the working class and the ranks of petty merchants into the professions and higher rungs of business. When measured against other white immigrants, those who arrived before them as well as their contemporaries, Jews did manage with greater speed to propel themselves upward, with one generation not replicating the economic profile of the one that came before it. For the most part, the project of comparative ethnic-mobility studies served no real purpose, but in this case, however, they did provide one important lesson.[25]

The Jews' long exposure to trade, to building communities around entrepreneurship, and relying on internal credit networks worked to their advantage when it came to being able to take advantage of American opportunities. For immigrants who came to America, that land inhabited by people who wanted to buy things, but doing so without long histories of trade and without built-in webs of communal economic support, mobility had to be won differently, much more slowly, and with greater difficulty.

One illustration of great magnitude may highlight this as it also illuminates the ways in which the economic experiences of the Jews and the needs of Americans converged for the benefit of the Jews. Jews, women and men, had for centuries made a living as tailors and seamstresses, sewing new clothing and remaking used clothing, indeed monopolizing the old-clothes trade. Countless millions sold what they sewed to the public, and probably an equal number labored for someone else, earning wages for another Jew, who reaped the profits of the needle work.[26]

The largest of the Jewish migrations to America, the one from eastern Europe, which began to germinate in the 1850s and 1860s and then took off with even greater velocity in the 1880s, stimulated by the technological development of cheap steam travel across the Atlantic, responded to the simultaneous development of the garment industry in America. The expansion of the garment industry, which would so powerfully transform Jewish history, began with the invention and patenting of sewing machines capable of industrial production by Elias Howe in the 1840s

---

25. Stephan Thernstrom, *Poverty and Progress: Social Mobility in a Nineteenth Century City* (Cambridge, MA: Harvard University Press, 1964); Joel Perelman, "Selective Migration as a Basis for Upward Mobility? The Occupations of Jewish Immigrants to the United States, ca. 1900," Working Paper 172, Bard College, 1996; Thomas Kessner, *The Golden Door: Italian and Jewish Immigrant Mobility in New York City, 1880–1915* (New York: Oxford University Press, 1977).

26. Adam Mendelssohn, *The Rag Race: How Jews Saved Their Way to Success in America and the British Empire* (New York: New York University Press, 2015).

and Isaac Singer in the 1850s, preceding the outbreak of the Civil War. As hundreds of thousands of men went into uniform, voluntarily or not, it became possible to calculate the ratio between body measurements—height and weight—with the amount of fabric a garment required, resulting in the emergence of standardized sizes.

Added to this, late nineteenth-century urbanization, the movement of young women into industrial and white collar jobs in the years before marriage, the rise of the advertising industry, the emergence of "style" as something within the reach of working-class women, new sanitary standards that defined as a necessity changing ones' clothes frequently, all led to the reality that by the end of the nineteenth century the garment industry took off as one of the most dynamic sectors of the American economy. American-made garments, churned out by immigrant labor, women as well as men, also helped fuel consumer frenzy, as each season required its own frocks.

Young women, devotees of the pastime of window shopping, used some of the money they earned as stenographers, factory workers, retail clerks, and other such occupations, and sought out the newest items as they tired of the old. Made cheaply, often in imitation of the high-end clothing worn by the well-off, these garments demanded a large, poorly paid workforce to rapidly produce new garments at relatively low cost. Factories, heavily although not exclusively housed in New York, sewed the garments that clothed women and men around the nation and, in fact, the world. The ready-to-wear clothing industry spread its dresses and blouses, shirtwaists, hats, and undergarments, coats and jackets, around the nation and the world, fueling American economic development and drawing Jewish immigrants to America.[27]

One small story might illustrate this. Ida Cohen Rosenthal, after a stint as an apprentice to a Warsaw dressmaker, came to America and opened a small dress shop in Hoboken, New Jersey. She ran it with her husband, William, making it into a modestly successful and not untypical store of its kind. The shop did do well enough, however, to allow the couple to move their operation across the Hudson River into New York City, the hub of the nation's clothing world. Here she gained a good sense of the business, of American tastes, and took advantage of the opportunities available to her. In the 1920s she saw something in the lives of American women that allowed her to launch a revolution in women's lives, something that would literally touch them every day. She recognized that while much of the new clothing being advertised and sold after World War I, a period of

---

27. As two examples of the robust literature on Jews and the garment trade, see Nancy Green, *Ready-to-Wear and Ready to Work: A Century of Industry and Immigrants in Paris and New York* (Durham, NC: Duke University Press 1997); and Susan Glenn, *Daughters of the Shtetl: Life and Labor in the Immigrant Generation* (Ithaca, NY: Cornell University Press, 1990).

economic prosperity for many, addressed the aspirations of young and slim women, those who conformed to the era's flapper ideal, of athletic shape and flat chest. Rosenthal thought about, however, the vast majority of women with less sleek bodies who also yearned for style and fashion and in 1921 with her husband and a partner formed the Maidenform company, essentially inventing the modern brassiere.

The meeting point between Jews and America via garment making could not have been more fortuitous. The decades surrounding the turn of the twentieth century, the era of the largest Jewish immigration to the United States, happened to be also the period of time in which clothing, particularly for women, became the most significant marker of personal status. Perhaps because so many women no longer lived on farms where by necessity they had dressed functionally and simply in order to collect eggs and milk the cows, or because so many women spent their city time going to work in offices and stores, or because magazines, billboards, and even the movies projected images of stylishness against which they felt they had to measure themselves, they opted for the purchase of clothing as a way of enhancing their self-esteem and image in the eyes of others. Reformer Ida Tarbell sneered at this trend in 1912, writing, "It sounds fantastic to say that whole bodies of women place their chief social reliance on dress, but it is true. . . . If you look like a woman of a set, you are as 'good' as they, is the democratic standard of many a young woman." Tarbell derided this as a "folly," but commented that in that "lies . . . the pitiful assumption that she can achieve her end by imitation."[28]

Imitation depended on the seemingly ceaseless production of inexpensive clothing, dresses and shirtwaists, blouses, and jackets, which in turn depended on a labor force, organized to spew these out. The emergence of the garment industry as the Jews' niche coincided with the reality that for most working-class people, new clothes offered the one thing that they could afford to buy regularly to satisfy both need and whim.

Jews had achieved and maintained a visible and dominating presence in this field, even before the transition of garment making to a form of industrial labor. Jews in big cities and smaller communities around America owned dry-goods stores, and in the backs of their stores, the shopkeepers, male and female, as well as relatives, usually newly arrived from Europe, sat and sewed garments to be sold across the counters up front. The names and narratives of store owners who made and sold clothing pepper the histories of most Jewish community in America, indeed all of them, from the 1820s onward.

Some such clothing entrepreneurs operated small establishments while some became grand department stores, palaces of consumption in

---

28. Ida Tarbell, "A Woman and Her Raiment," *American Magazine* 74 (1912): 472–74.

which selling clothing to women dominated the shop floors. Most of the department stores catered to middle-class customers, although some like Filene's in Boston made a name for itself with its bargain basement as a subterranean place where the less-well-off could participate in America's buying frenzy.

A few stores identified a market for selling clothes to the affluent. Mary Magnin, a Jewish immigrant from the Netherlands, suggested that her husband, a failed picture-frame maker, try to make some money by going out on the road peddling, while she would try her hand at a venture of her own. She established in relatively short order a lucrative business sewing and selling high-end children's clothes to San Francisco's elite. So successful, she launched a department store in 1876, I. Magnin, and by 1906 I. Magnin diversified its operation, opening shops in some of California's toniest hotels, recognizing that wealthy tourists would want to bring back presents to their children.[29]

At the other end of the scale, Jewish ragpickers traversed city streets, scavenging for used garments, with shouts of "old clothes," intoned in the accents of central and eastern Europe, adding to the cacophony of American urban life, and closely fixing the association between Jews and the making and selling of clothing. These scavengers of bits and pieces of used garments sold what they had picked up to Jewish tailors who transformed them into wearable pants and jackets and other kinds of garments that were attractive to workers who could not afford new clothing. In the period around the Civil War, Polish Jewish immigrants dominated New York's second-hand clothing trade, centered around Chatham Street, which not accidentally abutted on the vast Irish immigrant enclave of the Five Points. Cheaply made second-hand clothing sewn on Chatham Street by Jewish "slop shops" ended up on the bodies of slaves in the South.

By the latter part of the nineteenth century, particularly in New York, Jewish contractors hired Jewish subcontractors who entered into arrangements with newly arriving Jewish immigrants to put their bodies down in front of sewing machines in tenement apartments to churn out garments that would then be sold by Jewish clothing-store owners. These sweatshops began to consolidate into factories in the early decades of the twentieth century, as entrepreneurs decided that larger work spaces could produce more clothes, faster and cheaper.

But whether behind the store, in the apartment, or in the factory, the making of clothing functioned as a kind of Jewish in-group experience. In this production and employment sector Jews as bosses and laborers founded and helped create a niche that transformed their own history and that of America. Some of the factory owners, like those who produced

---

29. Jeanne Abrams, *Jewish Women Pioneering the Frontier Trail: A History of the American West* (New York: New York University Press, 2006), 123–24.

men's suits in the Chicago outfit of Hart, Schaffner, and Marx, had come from German-speaking lands, or their parents had, earlier in the nineteenth century. But a substantial number had emigrated from eastern Europe, as did the women and men whom they would employ.

While this may not seem particularly notable, it ought to be remembered that Jewish immigrants almost alone among the millions of other newcomers to the United States worked in massive numbers for employers from their own group. Most Polish, Irish, Italian, Hungarian, Mexican, and so many other immigrants who came to the United States to work labored for others. Those newcomers who went to work in steel mills, textile factories, coal mines, railroads, slaughterhouses, and the like had as their bosses primarily Protestant Americans, of some kind of British extraction, many with deep and long roots in the United States. Besides the owners, the managers of the factories, the supervisors on the shop floors, those whom the immigrants had to obey, also did not share their ethnic or national identities. Those who worked for Standard Oil, Ford Motor, Goodrich Rubber, Swift and Company Meatpackers, as just a few examples, shared no common religion, language, culture, or sense of connectedness to the factory owners who employed them.

Not so the Jews, who came to America and went to work in the garment shops. The Jewish women, for example, who made a living sewing and stitching in the Triangle Shirtwaist Company, and then died there so tragically in March 1911, labored not for "Americans" but for immigrant Jewish employers. Isaac Harris and Max Blank, known around New York as the "shirtwaist kings," had both immigrated to America from the Czarist Empire, had both gotten started like so many other Jewish immigrants hunched over sweatshop sewing machines in an apartment. Clearly Blank and Harris like so many other Jewish capitalists did not treat their workers any better or with any greater sense of communal responsibility than did Andrew Carnegie, Henry Ford, or any of the other employers who relied on immigrant labor. Intra-ethnic solidarity played little, if any role, in the economic success experienced by Jewish immigrants to the United States.

An imagined bond between Jewish workers and Jewish bosses may, however, have helped shape Jewish unionization, something that did have a measurable impact on the lives of the immigrant masses and a force that propelled their mobility. Jewish women and men, organizing in factories and across the industry, in the field of women's clothing through the International Ladies' Garment Workers' Union and in the men's clothing in the Amalgamated Clothing Workers Union, demanding that the employers heed their calls for better pay, humane conditions, and the right to engage in collective bargaining, did not approach their bosses with deference. Rather they and their allies, particularly the socialist-inspired Yiddish press, invoked the communal imperative that religious obligations meant that the Jewish employer class owed the workers by virtue of their common culture. They declaimed in their union activities the Talmudic imperative that "all of Israel are responsible one for the other" and commanded employers to recognize the demands of labor. They also enlisted the support of Jewish communal notables, Louis Brandeis and Louis Marshall among others, to lean on the employers and push them to accept, however grudgingly, union demands in the name of peace within the group, embodied best in the 1909 Protocols of Peace.[30] (Harris and Blank alone among the Jewish factory owners refused to sign the Protocols.)

While immigrant workers in all the other big industries also embraced the message of the unions, and some also opted for socialism as their political ideology, they trod a very different path as they confronted their employers. Their journey as such involved more struggle, greater violence perpetrated by the employers and the state that supported them, and took longer, in some industries not really succeeding until the New Deal.

So too, the very nature of the garment industry, the single largest employer of Jews in New York in the early twentieth century, made it a perfect venue for employment, profit, and mobility. This field with its relatively low need for start-up capital provided Jews with one of the few, indeed the only, route by which immigrant industrial laborers could move into the ranks of the employing class. The lowest rung of Jewish employers in garment making, the owners of the many sweatshops of New York, themselves relative newcomers, needed nothing more than the apartment they already lived in, plus a few sewing machines, an iron, some tables and chairs, and contacts with a contractor, yet another eastern European Jewish immigrant. Some sweatshop owners required that the workers bring their own machines and thread, cutting costs even further, maximizing the potential for profit. Even the garment factories that began to replace the sweatshops by the 1910s and 1920s tended to be smaller and required less capital than say, a steel mill or an automobile plant, making it possible for other Jewish immigrants to also transition from the one state to the other, or at least to imagine that they could.

Not that the Jewish factory worker did not face a host of risks in trying to make the move from being employed by someone to employing someone else, but as a field, this enterprise, which historian Moses Rischin called the Jews' *métier*, offered a very different kind of work life and future for the newly arrived than what nearly all other, non-Jewish immigrants, women and men, experienced. Non-Jewish immigrant workers, in the main, could assume that they would end their work lives as workers, not as bosses who themselves reaped the profit. They might over time come

---

30. Hadassa Kosak, *Cultures of Opposition: Jewish Immigrant Workers, New York City, 1881–1905* (Albany: State University of New York Press, 2000); Richard Greenwald, *The Triangle Fire, the Protocols of Peace, and Industrial Democracy in Progressive Era New York* (Philadelphia: Temple University Press, 2005).

to live better, with greater material comfort, but self-employment as an employer in the same field of work lay beyond the realm of the possible. Immigrant Jewish workers, most of whom did not achieve this either, could however reasonably envision such a future.[31]

This difference reflected the Jews' economic experiences, the structure of the field in which they worked, and the realities of the American economy, all three coming together in a kind of perfect fit. Such a conjunction could be seen well before the late nineteenth century, when the largest number of Jews began to immigrate to America. Indeed this dynamic can be seen centuries earlier as Jews took their first footsteps in the Americas.

The British colonies of North America and the Caribbean, like all colonies staked out by the various European nation states, existed largely to facilitate international trade. Those who ruled the empire sought overseas colonies as sources of wealth, as places from which to extract natural resources, the profits from which would benefit the metropolis. Those who oversaw the colonial ventures encouraged the settlement of men and women whose labors, whether agricultural, commercial, or artisanal, would grow the colony, foster trade, and generally add to the coffers of those who ran the colony, those who had invested in it.

Jews served their purposes, and as a group, although their number remained small, found themselves far from the bottom of the economic ladder. Their rights increased over time largely as they proved their value to Britain, to its agents in the various colonies, and to those who hoped to gain wealth from the colonies. These Jews, both the small group of Sephardim with their roots in the Iberian Peninsula and the Netherlands and the larger group of Ashkenazim from Poland who operated at the lower and domestic end of this international commercial network, helped do what the colonial authorities wanted, extract profit through the export of raw material and import of finished goods.

The pace of commerce between the "mother country" and the colonies as well as the importation of slaves from Africa created a highly lucrative and integrated Atlantic world of trade, designed to benefit various interests in Britain. Jews, particularly the Sephardim, with their long immersion in global business, tapped into their far-flung kinship diaspora with great skill, operating within a Jewish trading network that spanned Europe, the Mediterranean basin, and Africa, as they played their part in the forging of the triangular trade route, the eighteenth century's version of globalization.[32] They, relying on family and ethnic ties, bought and sold

---

31. Moses Rischin, *The Promised City: New York's Jews, 1870–1914* (Cambridge, MA: Harvard University Press, 1962), 61–64.

32. For an account of Jewish involvement in the Atlantic slave trade, see Eli Faber, *Jews, Slaves, and the Slave Trade: Setting the Record Straight* (New York: New York University Press, 1998).

for their own benefit and that of their various colonies, New York, Rhode Island, Georgia, and South Carolina, as well as colonies in the Caribbean. The ships they outfitted and invested in circumnavigated the Atlantic world. Others of them purchased the goods that came off the ships and then sold them to the public, men and women living on the edge of the world eager for some of the comforts of back home.

Just a few sketches of some individual American Jews of this era reveal the degree to which their skills and economic experiences provided a comfortable meeting between them and other Americans. Asser Levy, for example, who had asked Peter Stuyvesant to remove some of the limitations imposed on the Jews in the mid-1650s, including their exclusion from the lucrative trade of the larger colony of New Netherlands, prospered tremendously once the British seized control of the colony. He exchanged locally produced flour and tobacco for finished products that came off the ships, doing such a brisk business that he could buy substantial amounts of property; and upon his death in the 1680s, the estate records listed him as one of New York's largest rate payers.[33] Esther Pinheiro, a resident of Charles Town, in the Caribbean, maintained a brisk commercial relationship between her base on the island of Nevis and New York and Boston, plying the waters of the Atlantic with her ship, the *Neptune.* Pinheiro, a widow whose husband had been a freeman in New York, transported sugar and molasses on the *Neptune* to the North American mainland, and from there, trading with other Jewish merchants, brought back flour, lumber, European-made finished goods, and the all-important cod, the staple eaten by the slaves from Africa. A century later Aaron Lopez of Newport began his American career as a shopkeeper, and within a few years dealt in an array of goods throughout Rhode Island, hiring business agents in Boston and New York. While he handled a number of products, he achieved local fame and great wealth through the manufacture and sale of spermaceti, wax derived from whale oil that went into the making of candles. Within a few years of arriving in Newport, he developed substantial business holdings in West Indian commerce and then segued into the African slave trade, which he managed alongside his business in candles, chocolate, ships, rum, barrels, and textiles. In the decade of the American Revolution, in which Lopez happened to have opted for the losing side, tax records enumerated him as Newport's richest individual, twice as wealthy as the next person on the list.[34] In the mid-eighteenth century Myer Myers established himself as one of New York's most

---

33. Leo Hershkowitz, "Asser Levy and the Inventories of Early New York Jews," in *American Jewish History: Vol. 1, The Colonial and Early National Period: 1654–1840*, ed. Jeffrey Gurock (New York: Routledge, 1998), 233–68.

34. Eli Faber, *Jews, Slaves, and the Slave Trade: Setting the Record Straight* (New York: New York University Press, 1998), 135–37; Goodwin and Smith, eds., *Jews of Rhode Island*, 18–22.

sought-after silversmiths, fashioning expensive and aesthetically pleasing objects, highly prized by the colonial elite. His wealthy patrons may have found the exquisitely rendered silver works produced in Myers's workshop something of a consolation for having to live so far removed from England, where beautiful ware could more easily be acquired. Myers won the respect of the other silversmiths of the colony, all non-Jews, who elected him president of their guild, a notable event given the historic reality that Jews had for centuries been excluded from such bodies.[35]

Levy and Lopez, Pinheiro and Myers, notable individual Jews about whom details of their economic, civic, and religious lives have been preserved, may have been among the wealthiest of colonial America's Jews, but their lives and fortunes did not deviate so far from the norm. Jews, even in this period, an era in which life in America did not reject European hierarchies and limitations, became among the best-off white colonists.

While their political fortunes did not correspond to their economic ones, notable individual Jews entered into partnerships with non-Jews. According to tax records and such personal sources as the rich trove of letters written by New York's Abigail Franks, they lived well and socialized comfortably with non-Jews. Their economic lives and their social ones corresponded well.[36]

While not alone in fueling the development of the Americas, Jews, with their widely dispersed Jewish contacts, helped ensure that goods and capital moved from one point to the next. Jews in the American colonies gained acceptance in the eyes of both colonial officials and the vastly larger non-Jewish population for their contribution to the empire's riches, the investors' desire for profits, and the usefulness which the colonies could show to London-based officials and business interests. That usefulness derived from trade, and that happened to be something the Jews knew well.

From the middle of the nineteenth century into the earliest years of the twentieth, as the American white population moved westward to the continent's remote and least settled areas, families and communities of "settlers" articulated a desire for cosmopolitan goods. If families were to leave Massachusetts and Maryland, Georgia or New York, for Ohio, Kansas, Missouri, or Oregon, they had to know that when they settled down on the frontier, that region which historian Frederick Jackson Turner described in 1893 as the "meeting point between savagery and civilization," they would be able to enjoy a standard of material consumption

---

35. Howard Rock, *Haven of Liberty: New York Jews in the New World, 1654–1865*, in *City of Promises: A History of the Jews of New York*, vol. 1, ed. Deborah Dash Moore (New York: New York University Press, 2012), 35–36.

36. William Pencak, *Jews and Gentiles in Early America* (Ann Arbor: University of Michigan Press, 2005), 38–41.

not so different and not so much lower than they had known back home. The settling of the frontier, that iconic element of the American narrative, meant a mass population transforming those imagined empty and barren spaces into places habitable for white people, filling deserts, forests, and plains with houses and barns, which in turn called out for tables and chairs, mirrors and dishes, beds, feather mattresses, pillows, linens, and towels.[37]

The westward movement of Americans across the continent made it possible for the nation's commercial interests to gain access to vast stretches of uninhabited land that could be farmed, mined, and logged, after first having been scarred with miles of railroad tracks, cutting across mountains and rocks. The nation's penetration of the hinterlands, romantically and jingoistically hallowed as its "manifest destiny" and justified as divinely blessed, required capital. It also required women and men willing to work the seemingly endless expanses of land, to fell the forests, dig the mines, lay the iron tracks, and the like.

That expansion and peopling of the land also needed intermediaries willing to bring to these people the kinds of "stuff" that made it bearable for them to live in these undeveloped places. Tens of thousands of central and eastern European Jews met America on the shifting peddlers' frontier. In Europe and the Ottoman Empire, traversing the roads and selling goods constituted a nearly universal Jewish experience. Most Jewish peddlers occupied the bottom rungs of an intra-communal web of trade and did so for a lifetime, having followed their fathers' occupational experiences as itinerant merchants while their own sons did so as well, in their time.

Jewish men, well-acquainted with this kind of selling after centuries of life back home, turned their long-time, and despised, economic niche into an American opportunity. They, in fact, went out as peddlers to all the new lands in the Americas, the Antipodes, and Africa opened up by European conquest and settlement. But more went to America than anyplace else, as it constituted the Jews' best hope for making a living and then, using that familiar occupation as a path toward living much better than they had before.

What transpired as these Jews from Alsace, Bohemia, Bavaria, Lithuania, and elsewhere came to the United States involved a marriage between Americans' desire for consumer goods, including but not limited to buttons, thread, needles, curtains, eye glasses, pictures and picture frames, fabric and ready-made clothing, and the willingness of Jews to pick up the familiar peddler's pack and venture out to anywhere they could find paying customers, no matter who they were. A 1931 history of the state of Iowa declared to its readers, "Most of us whose memories reach back

---

37. Frederick Jackson Turner, *The Frontier in American History* (New York: Henry Holt, 1921).

to the pioneer period of Iowa, or the years immediately following recall the Jewish peddler, who frequented the cabins of the early settlers." The writer, in praise of those hearty folk who moved there from the East as well as from Scandinavia and in praise of the Jews, "the most remarkable people of whom we have a record," went on in his description of the peddlers of the past: "These peddlers and their packs, with their display of cheap jewelry, including tin horns, used by the pioneers to call the menfolk from the back fields, were among the first memories" he could call to mind when thinking of his childhood. From the succession of peddlers who came up to the door of his farmhouse, he went on to describe how his mother bought her table linens, "while the children," he added, "always looked forward with interest to the coming of the peddler." Commentators had similar, if less eloquent statements to offer about other parts of the United States, and the Iowa description aptly ended with the observation that after their peddling years, many became, "prominent business men in the growing towns and cities of Iowa."[38]

A difficult and miserable existence, peddling worked because the men who did it considered it the fastest, most effective way to earn enough money to reconstitute their families and settle down. Their narratives abound with complaints about their heavy packs, the miserable weather, whether hot or cold, and the tedium of life on the road. Anti-Jewish attitudes rarely show up in their recollections, and while they spared no words to talk about their physical difficulties and their loneliness, their lack of hostility toward them as Jews reveals much about the synergistic relationship between American consumers' desire for goods and the Jewish immigrant peddlers' willingness to literally go the extra mile to bring it to them.

We know from their life histories that when the Jewish peddlers graduated from selling from packs on their backs to hitching their wagons to horses, they carried stoves and ice boxes, furniture and other heavy objects, which women in every region in the country, in farm areas and in logging and mining camps, in textile-mill towns and on the suburban fringes of larger cities, availed themselves of. They sold primarily to women because they carried the kinds of goods that related to the home; and because they had to approach their customers one by one, in their domestic spaces, they had to acquire English as soon as possible, meeting America in its own tongue—or better, tongues—as they also sold, depending on the region, to speakers of French, Spanish, German, Polish, Swedish, Ute, Cherokee, or whatever language worked best in order to entice customers to buy pictures and picture frames, curtains, towels, hair pins, or watches.

---

38. Rubey Edgar Harlan, *The Narrative History of the People of Iowa* (Chicago: American Historical Society, 1931), 469–70.

In the description of how America met the Jews, the peddlers played a particularly distinctive role. They walked or rode the roads five days out of seven, only returning to some hub of Jewish life for the Sabbath. The other nights of the week they availed themselves, if they could, of their customers' hospitality. The beds in their customers' homes had to be more comfortable than the hard ground of an open field or a forest, or even the back of the wagon. Sleeping in the homes of these Americans, many of whom were themselves immigrants, exposed the Jewish peddlers to the languages, cultures, and attitudes of the people among whom they would someday settle down. They learned about American tastes and attitudes, its range of religious and political sensibilities, and at the same time, at night, after having eaten—or not, given that the food was not kosher— at their customers' tables, they also had to explain themselves to these Americans, where they came from and the meaning of Judaism and Jewish culture. This two-way learning process, forged by the Jewish peddlers, provided them and the Americans with an intimate, in-depth opportunity to meet one other.[39]

The Jewish peddlers, who went to every state of the union, who became fixtures of life in America's rural and exurban areas, got their goods from Jewish wholesalers, who got their goods from Jewish peddler-warehouse owners, who themselves depended on Jewish manufacturers who produced the goods that ended up in the homes of millions of American customers, native-born and immigrant, African American and Native American, all of whom depended on the peddlers, who would weekly knock on their doors, cross the thresholds of their homes, and open their packs to display a wonder of goods. In the process of engaging in these prosaic commercial acts, the peddlers helped create an integrated Jewish economy that served the basic needs of the expanding United States.

Nearly all of the immigrant Jewish peddlers eventually descended from their wagons, put down their packs, and set up shops across the country, selling sundry merchandise, operating junk yards and peddler warehouses. Husbands and wives ran these stores, with the men at times continuing to peddle while the women stood behind the counters and at the cash registers, interacting with customers.

Jewish-owned stores became fixtures of small-town communities in particular, but even in larger cities, Jewish merchants purveyed hats and socks, shoes and dresses, "gents' furnishings," as well as liquor, hardware, and all sorts of goods, selling to their neighbors, regardless of religion or race. The father of multimillionaire Julius Rosenwald, who would oversee the vast empire of Sears and Roebuck, operated a modest men's clothing store in Springfield, Illinois, as of the early 1860s. He had begun his life in

---

39. Diner, *Roads Taken*.

America a decade earlier as a peddler, having emigrated from the Bavarian town of Bünde. Writing back to his relatives in Germany in the 1880s he noted that business went well, and while Jews did not exactly occupy the same social plane as the Christians in the Illinois town, little in the way of *Rischus*, anti-Semitism, marred life for his family and the other Jews in the capital city, all of them shopkeepers.[40]

The concentration of Jews in owning shops did not come without the occasional price tag. In his seminal study of Indianola, Mississippi, John Dollard recounted the story of one white southerner who commented that Jewish visibility as shopkeepers was such that "if there is a Jewish holiday, you cannot buy a pair of socks in this whole country."[41] Similarly, activists in Chicago's Polish neighborhood in the 1930s mounted a campaign to promote their own entrepreneurial sector, charging that Jewish merchants had secured a virtual monopoly on the stores upon which *polonia* depended, and exhorted residents to *Swój do Swòdejo*, which can be translated as "Patronize Your Own."[42]

Whether or not it bred ethnic resentment, the concentration of Jews, many of them one-time peddlers, in small business provided a point of intersection between Jews and other Americans. Some of the former peddlers made the move from modest emporia to grand department stores, with Macy's, Rich's, Filene's, Gimbels, Goldwater's, Neiman Marcus, Kuhn's Big K, and I. Magnin just a few examples. Other former peddlers, with familiar names like Lehman, Seligman, Goldman, and Sachs, eventually sat at the head of major financial concerns. The children of the immigrant Jewish peddlers went far beyond their fathers, making substantial lives for themselves, whether in business or the professions. Julius Rosenwald, the son of Samuel Rosenwald, the immigrant peddler turned proprietor of a men's clothing store in the Illinois capital city, appeared in one list as the fifty-seventh wealthiest individual in all of American history, a highly exceptional case, but one that pointed to the upward trajectory through trade and the ways in which America and the Jews encountered each other through the mutually beneficial buying and selling of goods. Rosenwald, the son, achieved his wealth through his presidency and stewardship of Sears and Roebuck, a company he did not found but whose operations he perfected. In the process of doing so, he made it possible through the wonders of the company catalogue for Americans, wherever they lived, to have delivered to their front doors everything they could possibly want or dream of. The Sears catalogue, like the Spiegel catalogue,

---

40. Diner, *Time for Gathering*, 228.

41. John Dollard, *Caste and Class in a Southern Town* (Madison: University of Wisconsin Press, 1937), 128.

42. Dominic Pacyga, *Polish Immigrants and Industrial Chicago: Workers on the South Side, 1880–1922* (Columbus: Ohio State University Press, 1991), 224.

also associated with a Jewish immigrant with a past history of peddling, stoked Americans' fantasies of consumption, as if they needed any prodding in that direction, given the acquisitiveness and embrace of materialism that so defined them.[43]

Stories of Jews capitalizing on the historic confluence of their familiarity with trade, their family networks of commercial support, and Americans' great appetite for material goods can hardly be contained in these few pages. Such stories spanned American history from the colonial period and to the twenty-first century. Such stories should not be understood as chronicling Jewish contributions or evidence of Jewish ingenuity. Rather they demonstrate how history, family patterns, and American markets shaped the Jews' entry into the life of the nation.

The examples of this could go on and on, as America and the Jews connected with each other through the market place of things. Ruth Handler, for example, the daughter of Polish Jewish immigrants, worked through the 1940s with her husband in the field of plastics. The couple launched a successful furniture business in Los Angeles that made use of the newly created materials Lucite and Plexiglass. She combined her work in her husband's businesses, which included the Mattel toy company, which he had founded with a partner, with raising her two children, Barbara and Kenneth. In 1956 the Handlers went on a business trip to Germany, where Ruth happened to see for sale a plastic doll, Bild Lilly, marketed as a kind of humorous gift for adults. Bild Lilly did not have a child's body like most dolls did, and Handler saw something marketable in this. Such a doll, she reasoned presciently, would have great appeal in this new age of television; it would be marketed to the mammoth population of children born after World War II, the children of the baby boom, whose teenage years, shaped by teen magazines, rock-and-roll music, and products galore, became the subject of vast and contentious social, educational, and political discussion. Ruth Handler conceived, created, advertised, and sold the dolls, a male and a female, named for her children, Barbie and Ken. With these two she provided American youngsters, girls mostly, with models in plastic of their own budding bodies.

Americans, it might be said, met the Jews through I. Magnin's fine wares, as they donned Ida Rosenthal's undergarments, leafed through the Spiegel catalog, literally purchased their homes and everything in it from the pages of the wish book of Julius Rosenwald's Sears, and, when their daughters begged them, one of Ruth Handler's precocious Barbie dolls. Each one of these and their many counterparts helped stoke America's love affair with material consumption and came into being because of it.

---

43. Michael Klepper and Robert Gunther, *The Wealthy 100: From Benjamin Franklin to Bill Gates: A Ranking of the Richest Americans, Past and Present* (Secaucus, NJ: Carol Publishing Group, 1996), xii.

The engines that generated economic mobility for subsequent generations, particularly for the children and primarily the grandchildren of the turn-of-the-century immigrants in the mid-twentieth century, had less to do with trade and the production and distribution of material goods to sate Americans' desire than in earlier eras. Rather, in the post–World War II period, when society shifted to one that depended on literacy and complex knowledge and in which educational credentials mattered, Jews again found themselves situated at the place where their experiences and the thrust of the larger America melded together.

The decades after 1945 and beyond, the era dubbed "the American century," saw the movement of Jews into social work, education, the academy, law, and medicine, and the like. Behind this historic drama, and all the earlier ones that had been structured around Jewish trade and American materialism, lay many complicated economic and political developments, far beyond this essay.

But all of these convergences between, on the one side, Jewish history, with the Jews' deep connection to peddling, shopkeeping, and garment making, and, on the other, the needs and wants of the American economy can be seen as propitious encounters. Not that Jews in other lands did not also move upward economically and come to enjoy professional success, but so many more lived in the United States that it provides us with a singular story.

The history of Jewish encounters with America in the matter of money provides a perfect example of a group of people having made their way to the right place, at the right time, with the right skill set to be able to serve themselves and their American neighbors. That they met around this commercial nexus worked for both the Jews and for America.

5

The Politics of Tweedle Dee and Tweedle Dum: Jews and the American Party System

Socialist Helen Keller, well known for her triumph over her physical disabilities, offered a particularly harsh criticism of American politics. "Our democracy," she commented, "is but a name. We vote? What does that mean?" Keller then went on to answer her own question, "It means that we choose between two bodies of real, though not avowed autocrats. We choose between," invoking the little chubby men from Lewis Carroll's *Through the Looking Glass*, "Tweedle Dee and Tweedle Dum."[1]

As she saw it, American politics served the interests of capitalism, those who held economic power, and it did so by offering the voting public no real choices. After all, the two characters drawn by illustrator John Tenniel in the 1871 book looked exactly alike. They differed not at all from each other, and Alice, who stumbled through the fantastic wonderland of Carroll's book, could never tell them apart.

Keller, born in 1880, came to public prominence and began to participate politically in the early twentieth century, an era that coincided with what political historians have referred to as the "fourth party system." Despite several major economic depressions, the widening gap in incomes between the classes, massive immigration, urbanization, volatile labor upheavals, the farmers' revolt, which inspired populism, and the flowering of the Progressive movement, the two parties, her Tweedle Dee and Tweedle Dum, remained fixed in terms of constituency and ideology.

The Republican Party, founded in the 1850s as an inheritor of the earlier Federalist and Whig parties, did gain the upper hand during these years. But neither it nor the Democratic Party, with roots going back to the early new nation and Thomas Jefferson, changed appreciably. Neither did any serious labor party or worker's party emerge as a robust competitor to the status quo, challenging the ethos and ethics of capitalism.

---

1. As cited in Helen Keller, *To Love This Life: Quotations* (New York: American Foundation for the Blind Press, 2000), 79.

All officeholders, a few minor exceptions proving the point, on the federal, state, or local levels came from one or the other of the two parties, in Keller's time, before, and after. The political parties existed to elect men—later some women as well—to positions of public trust, from president at the top down to road commissioners, school board members, and aldermen at the bottom end of the prestige-and-power spectrum. Between elections the parties barely existed other than to make sure they could make a credible showing at the next election, but for the most part they did not spawn ancillary activities or institutions.

In European politics, with its parliamentary tradition, the multiple parties served more ideologically charged and narrower bases of voters than in the United States. There political parties sponsored athletic teams, club houses, youth groups, and held regular mass meetings built around the particular ideologies they espoused. In that system, which operates according to proportional representation, parties can do well but need not get the majority of voters. They therefore exist to serve their supporters. Some parties, particularly those associated with workers, maintained health facilities, vacation places, and a range of services to their *members*, a category of affiliation that did not exist in a meaningful way in the American system, where, for the most part, parties could claim *registered voters*.

Those parties in Germany, France, Italy, and elsewhere, by the late nineteenth century, pivoted around ideologies that deeply informed the stands they took on major issues of the day and reflected how they recruited and interacted with their supporters. In these places, for the most part, multiple parties jockeyed with one another as they sought to extend their influence. These countries operated along a parliamentary model. A united government led by a prime minister, the leader of the party with the most seats, managed the state and decided on its foreign and domestic policies.

Not so the United States with its winner-take-all framework and constitutional system of checks and balances, the separation of powers between the three branches of government, and its bicameral legislative structure in which, often, one party dominated one house and the other party controlled the other. Additionally, federalism, which invested much power in the states, weakened the ability of the central government to exercise authority, diffusing responsibility for policy making between Washington and the multiple statehouses around the country. The United States may be thought of as the perfect example of politics as the art of the possible, not the arena to achieve utopian ideals.

In such a structure, parties meant very little, and for most of American history, with a short hiatus in the early nineteenth century and the "era of good feeling," which saw only one party on the scene, the two-party balance prevailed. Particularly since the end of the Civil War and the undoing of Reconstruction in the late 1870s, as the federal government allowed southern states a free hand in subjugating their African-American populations, the two parties tended to converge ideologically. Once African Americans lost the vote with the triumph of Jim Crow, the Republicans and Democrats could basically pursue similar strategies, differing at their margins and not at their cores.

Both parties spent their time cobbling together fragile coalitions of interest groups, carefully calculated so as to, as much as possible, not offend any large regional, occupational, or ethnic group. Candidates running for office and the party operators behind the scenes had to craft messages that held these coalitions together as they always faced yet another upcoming election.

The two-party paradigm tended in the United States, and just about any other place that functioned with such a system, to promote centrist politics, defuse ideology, and seek out positions that did not deviate too far from one another.

Some political scientists and political historians have argued that this equilibrium promoted political stability, which in turn proved to be essential to maintaining the economic order. Others, scholars and political activists such as Helen Keller, whose words opened this chapter, lamented that it led to stasis, blunted the airing of alternative views on issues, stymied experimentation with new ideas, and made it impossible to advocate for needed, radical solutions. These critics have argued indeed that in a two-party system so committed to slow change through clumsy procedural plodding, apathy rather than political intensity prevails.

America's two parties have historically functioned without formal membership and only the vaguest of platforms, trotted out and tweaked every four years, announced at conventions, and then shelved until trotted out again during the next election cycle. While certain issues did divide the Republicans and Democrats, particularly in the late nineteenth and early twentieth centuries, the period of time when the largest number of Jews entered into the system, these issues for the most part did not generate intense ideological fire. The strongest and most solid base of the Democratic Party was concentrated in the South, which had effectively suppressed the voting of African Americans, while the relatively small number of African Americans who could vote leaned Republican. The tariff, advocated by the Republicans and opposed by the Democrats, also split the parties, along with the question of gold-versus-silver backing for money, with the Grand Old Party, the Republicans, favoring gold and the Democrats, influenced by the threat of two of the nation's third parties, the Greenbacks and the Populists, claiming silver to be better for the average American.

Despite party platforms, most party life in America has been issueless. Politics bred pragmatic majoritarianism. Much to the chagrin of those with political agendas, whatever their message, the nature of the political system frustrated any effort for real change. American politics have been, since the latter part of the nineteenth century, castigated by those eager to pursue important causes as utterly compromising, and voters got only a choice between two somewhat indistinguishable individuals representing somewhat indistinguishable parties.

What seemed to matter most over the course of much of American history in this kind of politics was simply who got the most votes. Elected officials, or aspirants to office, had to read something labeled "public opinion," the prevailing attitudes of the public on matters of concern. The invention of polling in the 1930s made it somewhat easier for those eager to get and hold office to ascertain what a majority of Americans wanted, but even before then those out on the campaign trail considered it important to never be terribly far off the mark of the will of the voters. Both parties engaged in this, and both for the most part tried to sell themselves to the same people.

Those people, that is, the enfranchised white men for most of American history, understood that they had something of value. They let those who wanted their votes know who they were, what they wanted, and how they could, often literally, be bought. One political scientist, Daniel Bell, offered a powerful image to think about this historic reality. American parties, he wrote, resembled giant bazaars, under whose canopies, multiple hucksters sold their wares. "Life within the bazaar," he wrote, "flows freely and licenses are easy to obtain." But he cautioned, "all trading has to be conducted within the tents; the ones who hawk their wares outside are doomed to a few sales." The same hucksters appeared in each of the big tents and peddled their goods, representing their issues, concerns, and agendas. The barkers in the twin bazaars represented the various interest groups: labor, farmers, manufacturers, various ethnic groups, and the like.[2] While both parties essentially served the interests of business, under the shelter of the two tents, the parties brokered among these constituencies. The parties wanted votes, and each group had a particular, and usually practical, agenda.

Those constituencies functioned as interest groups, agglomerations of men, and also women, who had a stake in the crafting of state policies on a variety of subjects. These interest groups used their numbers at the ballot box to influence those who decided how the government would conduct its business, be it vis-à-vis domestic or foreign matters. Each interest group took its case to the two parties and saw who made them the best deal. In exchange, the leaders of the interest group sought to mobilize voters, to reward the party that listened to them, and punish the one that did not. In

---

2. Daniel Bell, *The End of Ideology: On the Exhaustion of Political Ideas in the Fifties* (Cambridge, MA: Harvard University Press, 1960), 103.

one of the most succinct and insightful statements on this matter which so profoundly impacted the Jews, political scientist V. O. Key wrote in 1942:

> A striking feature of American politics is the extent to which political parties are supplemented by private associations formed to influence public policy. These organizations, commonly called pressure groups, promote their interests by attempting to influence government rather than nominating candidates and seeking responsibility for the management of government.

Using farmers and the activities of the American Farm Bureau Federation as an example, Key went on to say that they, as well as all other pressure groups, "are concerned with what government does either to help or to harm their membership. They do not attempt to assume, at least openly, the party's basic function of nominating candidates." Rather, they "supplement the party system and the formal instruments of government by serving as spokesman for the special interests within society."[3]

Substantial numbers of farmers and farm-based communities existed in many, indeed all, states around the nation. Farmers had their issues. Farmers voted, and while farmers split among themselves on a variety of important matters, of no real interest here, no politician in Wisconsin, Kansas, New York, Alabama, California, and so on could afford to alienate farmers as a group. Across the party divide, those eager to get elected to office had to court farmers and find ways to present themselves as friends of the farmer.

This tended to lead not only to the political wooing of the men and women who farmed but also meant that representatives in Congress, when it came to pending farming legislation, had to cross party lines and vote the same way, when they could, in support of bills that the farmers in their states and districts wanted.

Vis-à-vis this constituency and so many others, bipartisanship flourished. Democrats and Republicans could vote the same way on the floor of the Senate or the House and in their state legislatures. They had to, as the phrase went, reach across the aisle and cast their "yeas" or "nays" less by party line and more by their sense of what would get them elected next time around.

Both parties contained multiple wings, spanning ideologies. In the halls of government at the state and national levels, politics gravitated toward the center, as some Republicans and some Democrats had more in common with each other than with members of their own party. The mid-twentieth century saw the prominence, for example, of a substantial

---

3. V. O. Key, Jr., *Politics, Parties, and Pressure Groups*, 5th ed. (New York: Thomas Y. Crowell Company, 1964), 18–19.

number of liberal Republicans, individuals like Jacob Javits, senator from New York, or William Scranton of Pennsylvania, whose commitment to matters such as civil rights resembled those of some of the most progressive of the Democrats. On the other hand, the influence of highly conservative Democrats, particularly although not exclusively those representing the South, who put the preservation of racial segregation at the top of their agendas, meant that the Democratic Party functioned as a fractious house, divided within itself.

The parties, with their internal fissures, had to find ways to navigate all the sundry and often competing interest groups, articulated by farmers and other occupations, and by Jews, just as by other ethnic and religious groups, all seeking to be heard. The parties, both of them, always concerned with winning over as many voters as possible, had to walk a line between these elements of the voting public.

In such an arrangement, compromise and accommodation ruled the parties, and in all of this, politics, like religion, became tamed. America saw no party of the aristocracy or the clergy, of peasants or the urban proletariat. Rather each party sought to claim as many constituency groups as possible and had little incentive to offend any identifiable block and as such write off any potential voters.

The politics of offense and extremism fell into the domain of the third parties, each of which had its moment in the sun of the political landscape, engendered fear and concern among the operatives of one or the other of the two behemoths, depending on the issues involved. Third parties tended to focus on single issues. They managed at times to elect a few individuals here or there on the local, state, and even national levels, and then all experienced the same fate. They faded out and died. The Free Soil Party, the Anti-Masonic Party, the Greenbacks, the Know-Nothings, the Socialists, the Populists, the National Woman's Party, and others that achieved less visibility than these, all had some impact on the two giants by nudging one or both of the parties to adopt their rhetoric and even some of their leaders, coopting them and in the process rendering them superfluous. In paying lip service to this outlier party or that one, the Republicans or the Democrats managed to deflate extremism and steer politics back to the American middle course of compromise and consensus.

At times, third parties purposely sought to inflame public discourse against some element in the American population and built their political agendas around an ideological argument that some group or another of Americans harmed the nation and needed to be dealt with harshly. The Anti-Masonic Party, the nation's first third party, targeted Freemasonry and had a brief but visible moment, particularly in upstate New York, as it campaigned against the secret society, an elitist organization, which, the opponents of masonry complained, violated republicanism and egalitarianism. It purposely called out local Masons. More significant as a political force, the Know-Nothing, or Native American, Party of the 1850s considered the influx of Irish Catholics, starting the decade before the Great Famine in Ireland, a mortal threat to American democracy. The Know-Nothings campaigned openly against Catholics, the Catholic Church, and the Irish as agents of the pope, depicting them in party rallies, broadsides, and stump speeches as drunkards who took their orders directly from Rome. The Know-Nothings promised potential voters that if elected they would curtail Catholic immigration and engage in policies that would render the Catholic Church powerless on American shores.

The two parties themselves, however, shied away from such issue mongering, at least in its most blatant form, in part because members of Masonic lodges and Catholics represented substantial blocs of voters. While the Republican Party rarely got the Catholic vote until the middle of the twentieth century, the Democrats having sewn it up, the former had no reason to absolutely write Catholics off. Many Italian immigrants to the United States gravitated in fact to the Republican Party largely because the Irish, their coreligionists, ran the machinery of the Democratic Party, particularly on the local level in New York, forcing, or perhaps allowing, the Republicans to incorporate this new, large, Catholic population.

This matter also points to another factor that will help explain how the culture of American politics, and especially its issue-light, two-party system, winner-take-all structure, greeted the Jews, doing so in ways that led to integration. The sheer diversity of the American public, or better, of the white American public, meant that neither party could *ipso facto* alienate or write off any group of voters. Cities, states, and the nation as a whole consisted of a wide jumble of ethnic, religious, and occupational groups, all of whom had votes, and simply adding up the numbers meant that, unless cheating went on, all their votes counted.

The system worked well for all white immigrant men. Democratic politicians in New York and elsewhere could not but recognize the number of Irish newcomers arriving, becoming naturalized, and emerging as a powerful base of voters. Although reviled by so many Protestant Americans, their presence spawning the vocal and briefly successful powerful Know-Nothing Party, this group of immigrants not only got incorporated into urban politics but essentially took it over. Wherever they lived, Irish men plunged into politics, knowing full well that their whiteness allowed them to do so and that politics served as the gateway to jobs, patronage, power, if not eventually some respect.

The Irish, like so many other newcomers, Jews included, used their political presence to advocate for homeland issues, linking their numbers at the voting booth with efforts to get the United States to act for whatever the immigrants believed their country of origin, or their transnational community, needed. Many immigrants, after settling in the United States, maintained close connections to their places of origin and to their brethren around the world. They used their participation in American politics to enlist, successfully or not, the assistance of the United States in support of homeland causes. They understood that by acquiring citizenship and voting and lobbying as citizens, they could advance the needs of the places they had left but where they still had family and to which they felt an emotional tie. Polish communities in the United States, for example, worked assiduously in the years before, during, and immediately following World War I to get the United States to support the establishment of an independent Poland, a dream nurtured since the end of the eighteenth century. Dreams of national honor and independence spurred Irish American political action as well.[4]

But for Polish immigrants and their children in, say, Chicago or Buffalo, the issues involved in political participation transcended homeland independence. Parks, schools, garbage collection, relations with the police, street cleaning, securing city contracts, municipal employment for their sons and daughters, among other concerns, mattered day to day; and this group, the Poles, existed in constant competition with the Italian, Czech, Greek, and other ethnic communities, including the Jews, in these cities, who also wanted their voices heard and who also had their quotidian local concerns. This quest for visibility required being there and participating. All of them had to make their presence felt by voting, supporting one faction or another of the political machine, making deals, getting their men on committees and on the ballot, While no group ever approximated the urban Irish and its rise to political power, all white immigrant men recognized that the nature of American politics could serve them and their communities.

In large cities, where most Jews settled and lived, politics pivoted around the activities of the machine, the party organization that directed the provision of services and the garnering of votes. In the face of weak government involvement in the lives of average people, the poor in particular, the machine and its operatives, led by the "boss," stepped in and helped, expecting that votes from the grateful poor would make a difference when election day came around. The machine in New York and Chicago, the most important places for the Jews, started out in the early national period as a bastion of the native-born Protestants, but the Irish soon supplanted them as masters of the system. The machine, like New York's Tammany Hall, served over the course of the next century as a force for integrating the newly arriving male immigrants, never considering any group too small, too insignificant, or too hated to be ignored. Machine politicians, from the boss at the top down to the ward and block

---

4. For more on ethnic nationalism within immigrant communities in America, see Matthew Frye Jacobson, *Special Sorrows: The Diasporic Imagination of Irish, Polish, and Jewish Immigrants in the United States* (Berkeley: University of California Press, 2002).

captains calculated every vote and every voter as a potential contributor to its ranks.

Tammany's George Washington Plunkitt, practitioner par excellence of machine politics, granted a series of interviews to a reporter, William Riordan, in 1905, and those interviews bundled together in a little volume, *Plunkitt of Tammany Hall*, bore witness to the "practical politics" of city life that gave Jews their place of importance in the quest for votes. As Riordan enumerated Plunkitt's flurry of pressing activities in the ceaseless quest for votes, he noted that in a typical day, the boss at "3 p.m.: Attended the funeral of an Italian as far as the ferry. Hurried back to make his appearance at the funeral of a Hebrew constituent. Went conspicuously to the front both in the Catholic church and the synagogue, and later attended the Hebrew confirmation ceremonies in the synagogue." Later that same day, the boss, as he scoured the city for voters to charm, "attended a Hebrew wedding reception and dance. Had previously sent a handsome wedding present to the bride." Unless they had just arrived in America, her father, husband, brothers, and the male Jewish neighbors who had attended the nuptials all already possessed votes to cast at the next election. Likely they would remember the gift and the dance and the august presence of the busy political operative.[5]

Political machines did not do this just for the Jews. Plunkitt went to an Italian funeral also, as he did for so many others, regardless of ethnicity, religion, or race, if he decided that his presence at a wedding, funeral, confirmation, or any other such gathering would attract attention from enough men, and if that attention could be translated into votes. Eventually, machines in northern cities found ways to bring into their fold African American migrants from the South and immigrants from Puerto Rico and elsewhere in the Western Hemisphere. The machine did this not because of any ideological commitment to inclusion, not because of nascent feelings of multiculturalism, but because without being cognizant of the changing local demographics it would lose its clout.[6]

Not that the machine sought anything other than power or that it cared particularly about forging a multiethnic polity. It did what it did, passing out jobs, handing out favors, not to transform American society but to win at the polling place. So, too, in one place after another, local machines responded to the arrival of new groups and found ways to provide jobs, direct services, and positions of, usually low-level, prominence for the newcomers. Jews benefited greatly from this because in the various

---

5. *Plunkitt of Tammany Hall: A Series of Very Plain Talks on Very Practical Politics, Delivered by Ex-Senator George Washington Plunkitt, The Tammany Philosopher, From His Rostrum—The New York County Court House, Bootblack Stand, Recorded by William L. Riordon* (1905), 92–95.

6. Steven P. Erie, *Rainbow's End: Irish-Americans and the Dilemmas of Urban Machine Politics, 1840–1985* (Berkeley: University of California Press, 1988).

cities where they clustered, they had numbers, and numbers translated into votes. Not that their numbers amounted to anything approaching a majority, although in New York and Chicago whole wards could boast large Jewish concentrations. But even in smaller cities, St. Louis, Kansas City, Jersey City, and Boston, Jewish men with their votes in hand counted, and by counting they entered into the civic arena.

Political participation in this kind of system mattered to all immigrants, as it did to Jews, who benefited, differently, but benefited nonetheless from the two-party, interest-group, nonideological political culture. In nearly all paeans to America and its ability to integrate (white, male) immigrants, stump speakers and historians alike have cited the ease of the naturalization process for those of foreign birth and the fact that the political realm did not exclude anyone because of his religion. Vis-à-vis politics and governance, for nearly all of American history, not only did religion not matter in regard to naturalization, acquisition of citizenship, voting, and officeholding, but neither did nativity. With the exception of the constitutional requirement that the president of the United States needed to be native born, no barriers to political participation needed to be overcome for white men, and later women, regardless of how, or if, they prayed and where they had been born.

The U.S. government committed itself to this not just in the Constitution but in one of the earliest bills to wend its way through Congress; the Naturalization Act of 1790 extended the nation's hand to all "free white persons of good character." Clearly the legislation automatically excluded indentured servants, native people, slaves, free blacks, and those from the Asian continent, defined by law as nonwhite. In its initial form, the law merely required that men, white and free, had to live in the United States for two years, one of them spent in the state where they would petition to become citizens. After appearing before a clerk of "any common law court of record," the candidate for citizenship had to take an oath to support the Constitution and the nation, and with the oath taken, the ritual recorded, he could go out to vote, having been wooed by candidates from the two parties, both of whom needed his support. (In the late 1790s the Federalists tinkered with the formula, extended the length of time needed, but by 1802, with the passage of a new Naturalization Law, five years of residence became established and has not changed over the course of the past two centuries.)

Such an easily navigable system worked well for a settler society, a nation eager to attract able-bodied workers of a certain kind to do the work necessary for the economic exploitation of the huge land mass that stretched "from sea to shining sea." By the time the majority of Jews arrived, in the period after the Civil War, those men provided the fodder for factories, mines, and mills that stoked America's rise to becoming an industrial dynamo, shortly thereafter, the largest. While not all immigrant men became citizens, and those who sought to return to their places of origin with money in their pockets tended to have relatively low rates of naturalization, those immigrants who considered their journeys across the Atlantic a one-way phenomenon had every reason to begin as soon as they could to take the first steps toward citizenship.

Deciding to stay in the United States permanently meant, besides finding work and making a living, embarking on the project of carving out a place for oneself and one's family, and, given the salience of communal loyalties for most immigrants, for one's brothers and sisters with whom one shared the bonds of ethnicity. Conversely, ignoring the political process, while it did not necessarily make it impossible to secure a job and earn money, made communal defense harder, advocacy for any back-home causes less possible, and removed one important avenue by which immigrant outsiders could earn respect from the larger society.

Notably, the Jewish mass migration to America began in the 1820s and coincided with a period of time dubbed in the literature "the age of the common man." It ushered in the expansion of the electorate and the emergence of anti-elitism as a political trope. All white men could now vote, and the parties scrambled to win them over.[7]

This then provides another way of understanding how the Jews met America and how America met the Jews. In conjunction with the long reality of the two-party system, the emergence of broad-based voting coalitions, and the low level of ideology that operated in the political sphere, the ease of naturalization, the lack of any religious qualification, and the fact of foreign birth as no obstacle to participation helped facilitate the American–Jewish symbiosis.

For a start, neither party ever defined "the Jews" as a problem, but rather both wanted their votes, helping to explain in part why until the late 1920s Jews voted inconsistently, not clustering around one party or the other. While individual Republicans, or before the 1850s their predecessors, the Federalists and the Whigs, as well as individual Democrats made nasty, even defamatory statements about Jews, they spoke for themselves and not their parties. As to the dissemination of nasty and scurrilous comments about Jews by political figures, in and out of office, we have ample examples, reflecting either their own feelings or catering to what they thought some of their constituents believed. But none of these parties advocated in their platforms any policies that might even be remotely construed as targeting Jews.

Even as the immigration issue loomed in the 1910s and 1920s, as the nation moved headlong toward restrictions based on national origins, the political discussion did not highlight Jews as *the* group whose numbers

---

7. Edward Pessen, *Jacksonian America: Society, Personality, and Politics* (Urbana: University of Illinois Press, 1985), 1.

ought to be curtailed for the national good. The 1920s legislation harmed Jews, grievously, but neither political party made the Jews a matter of public discussion as they lined up for and against the legislation. Jews were not the only ones who testified in Congress against the legislation, nor did they emerge as the solo opponents, in their own name, of the radical change in American immigration policy. Italian, Irish, Polish, and other communal organizations spoke out, lobbied with their representatives, and issued statements of outrage at the policy, as did umbrella groups like the National Conference of Catholic Charities, founded in 1910.

Indeed, no candidate for national office ever did anything other than hope for the Jewish vote. Even if the words and behaviors of these politicians in search of votes might be dismissed as gestures, as purely symbolic, these symbols mattered, and politicians hoped that these symbols would translate into the coin of the political realm, namely, votes. The story of General Ulysses S. Grant's Civil War Order Number 11, a harsh decree calling for the expulsion of the Jews from the area under his command, can be effectively counterbalanced by his actions as president a decade later when he was elected as a Republican.[8] He relied heavily on the advice of his close friend Simon Wolf, a Jewish communal leader, whom he named Registrar of Deeds of the District of Columbia; and as president, because he and his party worried about votes, he not only visited a synagogue, the first to do so, but spoke out against anti-Semitism and attempted to put diplomatic pressure on the government of Rumania for the violence being perpetrated there against the Jews. It probably matters little if in his heart he did or did not consider Jews usurious, dishonest, and driven only by profit. What mattered in terms of American politics and the Jews was that their votes mattered and they got courted.

Because the two parties differed so little from each other and neither one made Jews as issue, both thought of the Jews as a constituency that mattered, from the local through the national levels. Although by the 1930s the largest proportion by far of Jewish voters solidly aligned with the Democratic Party, the Republicans never ceased to yearn for them. Until the late 1920s, in fact, the Jews had split evenly between the two parties, with a sizable minority in New York City, at least on the local level, casting their ballot for the socialists.

As late as 1928, when nationally the Jewish drift to the Democrats became manifest, the race for the top spots on the ticket in New York State demonstrated how both parties hoped to secure the Jewish vote, a phenomenon Jews always and disingenuously claimed did not exist. The Republicans nominated one Jew, Albert Ottinger, for governor while the Democrats put up Herbert Lehman in the second spot, as candidate

8. Jonathan Sarna, *When General Grant Expelled the Jews* (New York: Schocken Books, 2012).

for lieutenant-governor, giving prominence to another Jewish man, and demonstrating the exquisite balance between the two parties in terms of their quest for as many votes as they could get in the Jewishly rich Empire State. After World War II, the Republicans in the 1952 election pinned a great deal of hope on a possible Jewish embrace of Dwight Eisenhower, the military's liberator of Europe from the clutches of Hitler. Rabbi Judah Nadich, a Jewish chaplain in the European theater, much enamored with his former commander, tried to enhance Ike's chances of translating the admiration of his fellow Jews into votes at the ballot box by writing a book (which came out just after the election) titled *Eisenhower and the Jews.* One-quarter of American Jewish voters did pull down the Republican lever that year, and the Republicans never gave up the hope that in subsequent elections they could nudge the Jews from pushing the other one.[9]

Neither party wrote them off as potential voters, nor did either party refuse to provide them with some tangible rewards for voting correctly. From the middle part of the nineteenth century onward, Jews got incorporated into party politics, usually at the local and state levels, and Jewish officeholders, Jewish operatives for the parties, and Jewish political clubs popped up across the nation. Even in places where few Jews lived, the appearance of a Jewish man on a city council or on a county board of supervisors did not seem out of place. Many of those former peddlers, whose experiences played such a crucial role in integrating the Jews through their commercial activities which brought them into their customers' homes, became shopkeepers, and from their places behind the counter of the stores on so many Main Streets, they entered into civic and political life.

In one town after another, these Jewish dry-goods dealers, department-store owners, and furnishers of "gent's clothing" took an interest in civic life, becoming pillars of the civic order. Whether Democrats or Republicans, it did not matter. Rather, they sought to win over customers and from that easily segued over to winning over voters to support them in their bids for city councils, school boards, and other local political offices. Sol Levitan, one of the immigrant Jewish peddlers, opted for Wisconsin. He involved himself in statewide Republican politics in the early twentieth century, having opened his first shop in New Glarus after he left the road. Excited by the progressive politics of Robert LaFollette, Levitan, the heavily accented, Yiddish-speaking immigrant with roots in East Prussia, that is Poznan, and Ukraine, held a variety of government positions and then served several terms in the 1930s as treasurer of a state with a relatively small Jewish population. Other one-time peddlers and

---

9. Judah Nadich, *Eisenhower and the Jews* (Woodbridge, CT: Twayne Publishers, 1953); Lawrence Fuchs, *The Political Behavior of American Jews* (Glencoe, IL: Free Press, 1956), 83–98.

shopkeepers, used to serving the public by selling to them, transitioned into politics, hoping to serve the public by holding political office.

Similar stories, with different party labels, can be told from across the country, from the pre–Civil War period and into the twentieth century, running as a continuous thread through history, functioning as a common theme in terms of how America's political system greeted the Jews. In the early twentieth century, for example, Louis Glazier, a Latvian Jewish immigrant who set himself up, after a stint in peddling, as a store owner in Michigan's Thumb region, in the town of Kalkaska. A pillar of the civic order, he refused entreaties by several of his non-Jewish neighbors to run for school board, claiming that not only did he have so little education as to make the idea ludicrous, but that as a merchant he did not want to jeopardize his business by making decisions that might alienate customers.[10]

The Jews who opted for politics split for much of American history between the two parties, sensing that both worked for them. They realized that each party, in its way, hoped to woo the Jews over to its camp. By functioning in this bazaar-type setting, Jews could literally shop around and make their case to both parties on the local, state, and national levels. They, no different from Midwestern farmers, blue-collar workers, or "members" of nearly every ethnic and religious group, could see who would do the most for them in exchange for showing up on election day. In this nonideological political structure that quashed extremism, Jewish men since the middle of the nineteenth century (and then women as well by the end of the first quarter of the twentieth century) found ample space to join in the competition for the attention and rewards that accompanied political participation.

This nonideological, defanged political process did not help the Jews secure everything they wanted, just as no group, no segment of the electorate had an uncomplicated record in terms of always getting everything they considered vital. Irish immigrants in America and their descendants repeatedly turned to the government of the United States to help them fulfill their aspirations for the liberation of Ireland from its hated English overlords. They, for the most part, hit a stone wall, but not because of any political weakness. They, in fact, had become among the most-skilled immigrants when it came to the art of politics, but they achieved little on the homeland nationalism front because of the tenacity of America and England's special relationship.

Obviously the tragic history of American Jewry's mighty efforts and the quite limited results they achieved during the Hitler era to influence American policy stands as a great failure, indeed the greatest. American Jews, their leaders, their publications, and the Jewish masses as a whole,

10. For more on Levitan, Glazier, and others, see Diner, *Roads Taken*, 184–86, 206.

fearful of the spreading threat to their coreligionists in Europe, wanted some lifting of the harsh restrictions built into the nation's immigration policy. They considered that immigration to America offered the best way to protect some, or many, of Europe's Jews from Hitler's threats.

American Jews remembered how America had welcomed them and their progenitors. As Americans and as Jews they had imbibed the rhetoric of this nation as the "Mother of Exiles," and attempted as they could to nudge policy makers to enable substantial numbers of European Jews to find refuge in America as the specter of Hitler and Nazism ominously loomed over them.

The American public, as reflected in the polling data at the time, however, made it abundantly clear to members of Congress and to President Roosevelt that it had no interest in seeing any softening of the policy that made immigration difficult and restricted. Whether anti-Semitism factored in or not seems less relevant than the overwhelming reality that Americans did not want any immigrants who they believed would take jobs away from them. With so many citizens standing in bread lines and living on government relief, the thrust of public opinion expressed the belief that newcomers would compete for scant resources.

Unemployment and economic distress still ravaged much of America as the Hitler threat worsened abroad and as American Jews sought an opening of the closed gates. The United States had not recovered yet from the first phase of the Great Depression, which had struck in full force in the early 1930s, when it then suffered a second, deep recession in 1937. That recession rumbled through America just as Jews, the political elite, the press, and community groups across the religious and ideological spectrum anxiously tried to spread the word among their American neighbors about the extent of the violence being perpetrated against Jews in Germany, Austria, and Czechoslovakia, as well as the increasing physical and economic mayhem facing Jews in Poland. Americans, fearful of their own teetering economic position, worried that an influx of immigrants from anywhere would just exacerbate the widespread poverty being endured by so many.

While substantial numbers of Americans expressed sympathy for the Jews over there, that sympathy did not extend to wanting them right here. Additionally, some Americans not only did not express concern for the Jews of Europe, but individuals and groups arose in the 1930s who essentially argued that Hitler might be on the right track. Orators and publications, some politicians, and others in the 1930s blamed the Jews for America's economic woes. The radio priest, Father Charles Coughlin, broadcasting from suburban Detroit, drew a mammoth listenership from around the country as he ranted and raved about the Jews, about Roosevelt as their agent, and the rightness of the Hitler vision. It would have been unreasonable to imagine that in an economically challenged environment in which millions of Americans tuned their radio dial to hear these weekly broadcasts that politicians of whichever party would step forward and advocate for the admission of hundreds of thousands, millions, of Jews to America.

The near impossibility of using immigration to America as a way to rescue large numbers of European Jews reflected the reality that, from the mid-1920s until after World War II, the United States never put into place any kind of temporary refugee policy. It never formulated a way to alleviate situations of acute crisis abroad by allowing women and men into the country beyond the quota system. It made no exceptions, and either immigrants arrived according to the newly established procedures or they had to sneak in without documentation, coming illegally. At no time in that tumultuous twenty-year period did Congress or government officials unseal the quotas for humanitarian reasons. Essentially, vis-à-vis American law, there were no refugees for whom the decade-old policy could be eased.

Other matters also made it highly improbable that the United States would have acted affirmatively to aid the Jews of Europe. Even after war broke out in Europe in 1939, isolationism in America reigned supreme, just as Jews in America increased their anxiety over the fate of their kin, literal and figurative, in Europe. Born of their disillusionment with the military intervention of two decades earlier in World War I, most Americans, as measured by the polls, by letters from constituents to members of Congress, letters to the editors of newspapers, and the editorials themselves, indicated that they did not see Europe's war as the business of the United States. Roosevelt ran his unprecedented third presidential campaign in 1940 in part on the solemn promise that America would stay out of the fighting being waged across the ocean, in Europe's war, a war that Jews considered to be a war against them. "Your boys," he vowed to the American public, "are not going to be sent into any foreign wars," and while all scholars and biographers admit that he knew full well that he would never be able to carry through on that promise, he clearly blocked off any kind of early intervention that might have saved substantial numbers of European Jews. When the United States did enter the war after the attack by Japan on Pearl Harbor on December 7, 1941, for the most part, the fate of the Jews of Europe had been sealed.

At no time before or after did American public opinion and the concerns of its Jews deviate more widely. The chasm between the two played itself out in the close to total impotence of American Jews to use their clout, their high levels of voting, and the prominence of so many of them, to nudge the system to work for them. Few politicians, needing to stand in front of their constituents in the always looming next election, wanted to present themselves to the voters as someone who had made it possible for Jewish refugees to come to America.[11]

In this failure, Jews, similar to other interest groups, particularly those that represented ethnic and immigrant communities, got little when their agendas departed from the full force of public opinion, from the built-in desideratum of the parties and the politicians to offend the fewest number of people.

When the agendas of American Jewry and American society as a whole came close together, a very different history came into play. Two examples can illustrate this. The very successful effort of American Jews in the 1970s and 1980s to enlist the U.S. government in their efforts to facilitate Jewish emigration from the Soviet Union can be seen as a happy marriage of convenience between Jewish global politics and American anticommunism. The robust and extensive support, diplomatic, financial, and military, of the United States for the State of Israel represented a second instance in which what American Jews wanted and what Americans as a whole defined as in the interests of the United States worked together.

By the beginning of the twenty-first century American Jews eager to wear their love of Israel on their sleeves, or more accurately on their lapels, brandished pins bearing the image of entwined American and Israeli flags. Those pins said it boldly, and in the case for Israel as in that of advocacy for the Jews of the Soviet Union and their right to emigrate, American Jews and American politicians from the two parties at every level of government demonstrated their mutuality of interest. The politicians, ever dependent on voter approval, sensed that their constituents, the great non-Jewish majority, agreed with them on these matters and that in their support of the Jewish agenda they did not deviate from the will of the broad American public.

While not minimizing or dismissing the tragic consequences of the Nazi and World War II era, the hurly-burly of the political marketplace made it possible for Jews in America to get some of what they wanted. Indeed, they got enough to believe that the system worked for them. They succeeded often and visibly, and this allowed them to feel part of the civic whole and to believe in the basic goodness of the nation. Jews learned that they could enter into election cycles—local, state, and federal—with a sense of certainty that they would be listened to, no less than others; and while they may have considered their case to be more compelling than that articulated by anyone else, they did not have to dread politics as a

---

11. A large and contentious literature on this subject exists, replete with much finger pointing and accusations. But the best, most deeply researched, most nuanced, and sober analysis can be found in Richard Breitman and Allan J. Lichtman, *FDR and the Jews* (Cambridge, MA: Harvard University Press, 2013).

social drama in which they could expect to be targeted as the source of controversy, as a problem to be solved.

American politics, light on ideology other than the support of capitalism, its Tweedle Dee and Tweedle Dum party structure, and its valorization of interest-group advocacy as the route to electoral success, helped normalize Jews. In becoming normal they could enjoy their privileges, including those that accrued to them by virtue of their skin color.

Helen Keller's disparagement of American politics as involving few meaningful issues, as represented by the two twins, worked well for the Jews. Tweedle Dee and Tweedle Dum might in fact be considered friends of the Jews and facilitators of America's encounter with them.

Last Words

The Historic Contexts of Greetings

America's unshakable two-party system, as well as the importance of being white, the valorization of religion as a positive good that made individuals and society more moral, the long tradition of immigration, and the incessant desire of Americans for material goods made America an attractive place for the Jews. Jews arrived into an environment that synergistically worked well for them.

Other places in the world displayed some or many of these attributes, and those places—England, France, Canada, Australia, South Africa, among others—also provided attractive homes for the Jews of the modern era who sought new places to live. Jews indeed did well in those lands, achieving economic comfort, physical safety, opportunities for political participation, as well as the chance to live as Jews in communities reflecting their values and communal will. But so many fewer of them went to any of them or to all of them combined in comparison with the number who chose the United States.

Size mattered, and because of their sheer numbers, the Jews of the United States created and occupied the single largest diaspora Jewish community in all of history. It came to be not just another home for Jews, like so many others around the world. Rather, it achieved eminence as the center of the modern Jewish diaspora. The United States, and not Canada or Argentina, not England or Australia, entered into the annals of Jewish history as a place akin to Babylonia before the Common Era, medieval Spain, and early modern Poland, a powerful center of Jewish life whose influence radiated far beyond its borders.

Size mattered in other ways as well. No other place to which Jews went during the great age of migration occupied as large an accessible land mass which lay open for economic development and in which the arriving Jews could fan out and deploy their commercial networks. They easily navigated the vast territory that opened up to them and to other white people, a territory with no real equivalent elsewhere in the world.

Size also came into play in making possible the Jewish–American meeting inasmuch as no other economy in the world took off as intensely and generated as much growth and capital accumulation. By the time the largest masses of Jews began to leave eastern Europe, the American economy had flowered so dramatically as to inspire both the romance and reality of nearly limitless possibilities. More Europeans and others calculated that America, more than any other spot on the globe, held out realistic chances for material success, and more of them chose America over anyplace else. When it came to the lure of migrating from an old familiar place of limited options to a new one in order to improve one's lot in life, no place equaled America, and Jews joined in that quest. For the most part, the calculus of their migrations paid off. That in turn only enhanced the draw of America for those eager to join the flow.

Size mattered as well because of the magnitude and diversity of the immigrant flood, representing so many people from such a wide diversity of places. Those others, the majority, arrived in America with the Jews and shared with them so many experiences. The welcoming capaciousness of the United States, certainly bred of the need for white labor, counted heavily in the encounter between America and the Jews. The great hall at Ellis Island and the other immigrant-receiving stations rang with a multiplicity of languages, changing over time as the source of the immigration changed; the cacophony of tongues resounding there and on the streets, in the hiring halls, the schools, parks, and other civic space made Yiddish, for example, just one more foreign language, not so different from Norwegian, Lithuanian, Czech, Greek, and so on. The fact of America as a migration destination certainly made it different from Hungary, Austria, Germany, Russia, or the other countries where Jews had lived for centuries. As sending societies, these places contended with the outward migration of so many of their people, not just Jews.

These places also experienced vast internal movement, but most migrants there tended to go from the imperial hinterlands to the larger cities, never needing to change citizenship, adopt new national loyalties, or in most cases not having to acquire new languages. They moved relatively short distances. Overseas migrations, however, differed in degree and kind.

Jewish immigrants and their children in America joined in the competition for resources with the other newcomers, all playing according to a script shaped by matters of politics, economics, and race. The other receiving societies to which Jews went—Argentina, England, Cuba, and Australia, among others—attracted many immigrants, but they came from a narrower range of places than those who came to the United States; and the Jews in those places had fewer fellow immigrants enduring the same ordeals of transplantation.

The breadth of the religious denominations that flourished across America, also essentially a matter of size, impacted the meeting. Too many religions existed in proximity to one another to make any one of them, Catholicism in the nineteenth century excepted, deemed unadaptable to the American environment. The existence in any town or in any urban neighborhood of lots of churches and a range of other religious structures, synagogues included, meant that all of them together made up the local landscape of faith. For the most part, Americans defined this pluralism of religious communities as a good thing and something necessary to the nation's economic prosperity.

Each of those matters, as well as the Jews' qualification for citizenship by virtue of their whiteness, deeply informed what they found in America. These factors shaped their meeting with America, doing so in particular ways. These same factors did not exist similarly in the other places Jews lived in the modern era, which means that the histories of those other places must be told around a different set of factors, each idiosyncratic to it.

This should not be seen as either boastful pride in America or ignoring the rich histories of Jews in all those settings and places. Nor should it be seen as patriotic rhetoric that ignores the ugly realities that ran through that past. The United States, for example, had at its command such a broad expanse of land because Americans and their government had no problem stealing it from the people who lived there and dealing them one savage blow after another. White people, immigrants and native born, could bask in the privileges of citizenship in large measure because those defined as nonwhite experienced every manner of brutality and exclusion.

All too frequently invoked patriotic paeans to American freedom, easy to digest, explain little about how and why a particular group, in this case Jews, chose to migrate to a specific country and how that migration led to a particular encounter. Without interrogating what freedom meant in the context of how those men and women faced America and how America faced them, the term serves a jingoistic purpose but does not advance understanding. The freedom trope sits well with Americans, who, like most peoples, like to think of themselves or their country as particularly good and particularly moral, specifically in comparison to other places.

In much of the historical scholarship and in the American Jewish communal discourse much has been made of the Jews as the authors of their own American destinies, as people who owed their good fortunes to their particular repertoire of skills and strengths. To say that they conveyed the appropriate cultural baggage, including literacy and numeracy, long histories of migration, and their tight-knit communities and families, barely skims the surface in trying to answer the question of why they, for the most part, did so well in America. That particular explanation tends to fuel Jewish ideas about their own virtues. It involves mainly unanalyzed, empirically deficient statements that Jews did better than others, and did so by their own efforts.

These two themes, the Jewish and the American, have converged over the arc of American Jewish history. American Jewish communal leaders as well as many who have contributed to the writing and presentation of that subject have engaged in double valorization. As Jews they have engaged in a process of communal self-congratulations, and as Americans they have pointed out the virtues of their land of choice. As to the latter, they may have, especially when it came to facing the larger American public, used this rhetoric as a way of demonstrating their patriotism, showing other Americans that they too could wrap themselves in the flag.

More prosaically, it is fair to say they arrived in a large enough, but not too large, number to be able to thrive, to build the communities that they wanted, to take advantage of fundamental realities that often worked to the disadvantage of others, and to apply their economic skills sharpened in very different environments to American material realities. The fact that they did not pose any kind of numerical threat to the Christian majority population meant that no one had to fear them as challengers to the established order.

The five factors sketched out in this book may not, in the end, be the stuff of celebration, and they probably sound less stirring than invocations to freedom. But hopefully they offer a way to think about what this particular history involved and why it developed the way it did.

Thinking about the confluence of these historical factors may also provide a cautionary note about the present. As realities they may not always be with us, and a new kind of America very likely may be in the process of eclipsing the one this book highlighted. Even before the 2016 presidential election, ominous clouds had begun to gather on the civic landscape, suggesting that a radically new kind of America could be in formation.

As to the economic prospects of the nation, the dynamism and the possibility, however imperfectly realized, that individuals could experience upward economic mobility may have come to an end. Economic growth has slowed, and much of the discourse in the press and the academy has pointed to stasis and even a downward spiral. Jobs for the technologically savvy, white, well-educated, privileged, and affluent may still be there in abundance. But large numbers of Americans find themselves unemployed, underemployed, and eking out their living doing work that offers not only low pay but no security, no prospects for growth, little chance of permanence, no protections, and increasingly no benefits. Deindustrialization and the vicious attack on labor unions launched by capital have left their mark on growing numbers of Americans. Fewer of them, when it comes to their economic futures, seem to feel a stake in the stability of the system. As so many see it, that system has left them behind.

The politics of compromise in the context of nonideological vote-getting strategies has been pushed aside in recent years by the emergence of a much more sharply divided and ideologically driven reality. Not only have moderate Republicans faded from the scene, but groups like the Tea Party have made purity and extremism the order of the day. Well financed special interest groups and lobbyists representing, for example, the National Rifle Association have made the will of the majority subservient to the wads of money they can spend, buying votes in legislative bodies, in city councils, state legislatures, and in Congress as well. So too religion has for several decades now stopped functioning purely as a blessing of individual choice. It has become less a matter of sustaining congregations of believers in their voluntary communities of faith. Rather, religious groups now seek, and have already been successful, in enlisting government to endorse their creeds, essentially imposing their values on the rest of society.

Rumblings from the political right declare that the U.S. Constitution ought to be replaced by a more up-to-date document. They declare, unashamedly, that they would like to see the Fourteenth Amendment, with its promise of birthright citizenship and due process, and the guarantees of the First Amendment jettisoned. Worrisome signs appear of the potential for the calling of a new constitutional convention that could gut, or replace, the government document that has been in existence since 1790 and that shaped the encounter between America and the Jews. Some who would like to see a new constitution consider this an opportune moment to reopen the issue of the United States as a Christian nation, a desideratum of some Christians a century or more ago, which Jews believed had been long laid to rest.

I have written a book that essentially tells an upbeat story. My positive assessment of the points of intersection between America and Jews emerged not by design but rather because that seemed to me where the evidence led. I stand by this analysis, however exceptionalist it might read. America's meeting with the Jews produced a history with little precedent, no equivalent.

In this book I have offered my scholarly assessment of the past, an analysis of eras gone by. Having written this history, however, I am with some trepidation also drawn to commenting a bit, as a conclusion, about the present moment, and even speculating tentatively about the immediate future. Knowing full well that historians ought not make bold pronouncements about matters that they have not studied in depth, I want to end this volume with my worries about contemporary America.

The America that evolved and that met the Jews may in this, the second decade of the twenty-first century, be poised on the brink of a revolution. An era seems to be dawning, with links to the nation's past, that has little admiration for fair play and disdains the changes brought about with the Civil War, the Fourteenth Amendment, the Progressive Era, the New Deal, and the Great Society, with their broadened protections for individuals and expansions in accepted definitions of citizenship.

All of these historic movements and events, fraught and imperfect in their own ways, however, moved America toward greater levels of inclusion and toward a belief in the principle that the state should exist, in part, to assist those with the fewest resources and to extend rights to those who had been bereft of them.

Those who are now capturing the headlines and calling for change consider the hard-won, and hardly fulfilled goals of the civil rights movement, of feminism, the struggle for gay rights, advocacy on behalf of the disabled and activism to protect the environment obstacles to their own quest for power, wealth, and status. In this early twenty-first-century moment we can see how Congress and so many state houses have embarked on multiple campaigns to chip away at the enlargements of democracy and to roll back progress made toward greater human rights.

Amid the angry voices shouting at us, with their strident demonization of immigrants and of Muslims, of African Americans, of those outside of the heterosexual norm, and of women, explosive chants about the "Jews" as villains and as agents of liberalism can be heard disturbingly often.

I obviously cannot speculate on where this will lead; nor do I know if this threatened revolution is real. But it has certainly already left its mark on civic life and public discourse. How it will impact America's Jews obviously cannot be answered. But suffice it to say that the new political realities lay bare the contingency of American Jewish history. The good fortunes of the millions of Jews who chose to migrate to America, exceptions and complications noted, depended on the existence of a particular kind of civic life and national culture. Those may be on their way out.

The details of the history of how America met the Jews by definition reflected the nature of American society, one that evolved slowly but developed in a way that made for a positive encounter. Not that that history lacked difficulties and unpleasant encounters, not that Jews did not experience torrents of ugly words and discriminatory practices, but those paled in comparison to the larger context of the welcome they received. The next chapter in their history may someday be written, and some historian in the future will have to think about how the dangers of the present, early twenty-first-century moment, left their mark on this group of people who benefited so much from a particular kind of America.

Index

142   *Index*